Developing Professional Skills: **Bankruptcy**

Lois R. Lupica
Maine Law Foundation Professor
University of Maine School of Law

Margaret Howard
Law Alumni Association Professor of Law
Washington & Lee University School of Law

Series Editor: Colleen Medill

WEST ACADEMIC PUBLISHING

444 Cedar Street, Suite 700
St. Paul, MN 55101
1-877-888-1330

Printed in the United States of America

ISBN: 978-1-63460-254-9

To Tom, Noah and Jesse, the most fun family ever.
– L.R.L.

To William Miller Howard, Jr., in memory.
–M.H.

Preface

THIS BOOK IS DESIGNED to give you the type of assignments you can expect to receive as first or second year associates. These assignments range from thorny questions requiring analysis of the law and memo drafting, to reviewing and proofreading a motion "sloppily" drafted by another lawyer. Although these skills are not typically taught in law school, they are indispensable in practice. The exercises and their focus have grown out of many conversations with practicing attorneys and judges.

The book includes 12 exercises, some substantive and some extremely practical. The exercises will expose you to the bankruptcy forms as a way of getting you to think about the information required to be disclosed in a bankruptcy case and the big picture issues implicated. The exercises are also designed to get you to write, and write and write, in a variety of contexts, for a variety of audiences. The exercises hone in on the importance of being both diligent and meticulous. They provide guidance, by way of example (for instance, the two chapter 11 motions in Exercises 11 and 12 found on www.developingprofessionalskills.com). This book is not substantively comprehensive, but it is not meant to be.

Each exercise requires you to keep track of and "bill" your time. In a number of instances, we have given you your billing rate, and asked you to justify charging your client "X" amount. Particularly in consumer bankruptcy practice (but also in business practice, which may involve intense fee scrutiny) it is important to be mindful of how much a task, project or issue costs to resolve.

We urge you to consult the ABA's Model Rules of Professional Conduct, which are readily available on the American Bar Association's website. These Model Rules are similar (or even identical) to the rules governing legal practice in most states. We think it is good practice for you as a student (and as a soon-to-be lawyer) to regularly consult the ethics rules. We ask you to read the Rules before every exercise that involves "interacting" with a client, paying particular attention to the following rules: 1.0, 1.1, 1.2, 1.4, 1.5, 1.6, 1.7, 1.13, 1.14, 1.16, 2.1, 3.1, 3.3, 3.4, 4.1, 4.3, 5.1, 5.2, 5.4, 8.3, and 8.4. Also, our Appendix includes an excerpt from the American Bankruptcy Institute's Ethics Task Force Report on 'Competency for Debtor's Counsel.' You should use this Report as a review and point of reference when thinking about the skills you need to competently practice bankruptcy law.

We consulted with a number of practicing lawyers and judges in preparing these exercises. We would like to thank Hon. Michael Fagone, Bankruptcy Judge in the District of Maine, James H. Cossitt, bankruptcy lawyer in Kalispell, Montana (and a member of the ABI Ethics Task Force), Richard P. Carmody, of Adams & Reese LLP in Birmingham, Alabama (also a member of the ABI Ethics Task Force), and James Molleur of Molleur Law in Portland, Maine. We would also like to thank Christine Iaconeta, Director of the Garbrect Law Library at the University of Maine for her invaluable assistance, Deborah Lorenzen for extraordinary administrative support, and Rachel Petersen, Maine Law '17 for excellent research assistance.

Table of Contents

FOR SALE

Developing Professional Skills:

BANKRUPTCY

CHAPTER 1

The Means Test: Consumer or Business Debt?

- **SUBSTANTIVE PROBLEM/TOPIC:** Consumer Practice; The Means Test and the Presumption of Abuse

- **LEGAL RULES:** 11 U.S.C. §§ 707(b), 101(10A), 1325(b)

- **SKILLS:** Drafting a memo to file; Preparing to file a Petition; Recording time

- **STUDENT ASSIGNMENT:** Prepare a Memo to the File addressing the best course of action for Mr. Lasiter, and if appropriate, complete Form 122A-2 or Form 122A-1Supp.

- **CLIENT BILLING NUMBER:** 48920.001

FACTS: You are an associate with a small bankruptcy firm that handles both consumer and business bankruptcy cases. It is a busy practice, and you are often asked to research a range of issues and provide your recommendations. Last week, you met with Mike Lasiter, and he told you the following story.

Lasiter, 37, owns a dry cleaning business (as a sole proprietor) and lives with his mother. He has approximately $200,000 in credit card debt, including almost $40,000 incurred to buy hangers, collar stays and gallons of perchloroethylene, the chemical used in dry cleaning.

He also has $20,000 in tax debt, owes $40,000 to his ex-wife in back alimony payments, and two mortgage loans secured by his residence (which he thinks is worth about $300,000). One mortgage loan is in the amount of $100,000, which he used to purchase the house, and the second one, in the amount of $145,000 was used to pay a graphic designer for his company logo and for a radio advertising campaign for his business. He also has a student loan balance of $35,000.

Lasiter has a gross income from his business of $4,000/month, and has monthly expenses of about $2,800. His mother's only income is from Social Security.

Lasiter tends to use cash for many of his business and personal expenses and often pulls cash from the registers before he leaves work each day. He has few assets of value, beyond the house, and a negligible amount in his bank account. Lasiter, who has never been good at staying on a budget, wants to know if Chapter 7 bankruptcy can help him.

Write a memo to the file, analyzing Lasiter's situation and recommending a course of action. If necessary, you should run a "means test" calculation in order to provide appropriate legal advice.

Be sure to record your time. Your billing rate was recently raised to $195/hour. How much did this advice cost Mr. Lasiter? Do you think you will be able to collect your fee? All of it? Does it depend upon the answer you reach and the advice you give Mr. Lasiter?

Points to Consider:

1. In analyzing whether a debt is a consumer debt, or a business debt, bankruptcy courts have developed a "profit motive" test: if the debt was incurred with an eye towards making a profit, then the debt should be classified as a business debt.

2. The character of the debt is determined when that debt is incurred, says the majority of courts that have ruled on the issue.

3. If more than 50% of the debtor's debts are non-consumer debts, the debtor is automatically eligible for filing a Chapter 7 case without having to bother with the means test. There is no presumption of abuse in such cases. *See* In re Kelly, 841 F.2d 908, 913 (9th Cir. 1988).

4. Would you automatically advise this client to file for Chapter 7, just because he is eligible and told you he has never been successful at staying on a budget? Are there some circumstances under which Chapter 13 would be more beneficial? Think about the pros and cons of each Chapter.

The forms below can be downloaded at http://www.uscourts.gov/forms/bankruptcy-forms for use in conjunction with this exercise:

- Official Form 122A–1Supp–Statement of Exemption from Presumption of Abuse Under § 707(b)(2).
- Official Form 122A–1–Chapter 7 Statement of your Current Monthly Income.
- Official Form 122A–2–Chapter 7 Means Test Calculation.

Time Sheet

DATE	CLIENT NAME	CLIENT BILLING NO.	DESCRIPTION OF WORK	TIME SPENT

CHAPTER 2

The Petition and Chapter 13 Plan

- **SUBSTANTIVE PROBLEM/TOPIC:** Filing a Chapter 13 case.
- **LEGAL RULES:** 11 U.S.C. §§ 1322, 1325, 342(b), and 707(b)(4)(D).
- **SKILLS:** Preparing a Voluntary Petition and Chapter 13 Plan; Recording time.
- **STUDENT ASSIGNMENT:** Analyze facts gleaned from client interview. Prepare Bankruptcy Petition, Schedules and Chapter 13 Plan.
- **CLIENT BILLING NUMBER:** 602640.001

FACTS: You are a new staff attorney in a general practice law firm. Your first appointment this morning is with a couple, Martha G. and Henry A. Valencia, who said on the phone that they were in financial trouble and were interested in finding out if bankruptcy can help them. They also told you that they were extremely upset that they even were thinking about bankruptcy; until Martha became ill and had to stop working, they had always paid their debts on time and in full. Largely because of Martha's health problems, their debts are currently overwhelming. They never thought that things would get so bad that they would have to consider bankruptcy relief.

During your initial meeting, you learned the following:

Martha and Henry have been married for over 18 years, and have one child, Miranda, age 15. They rent an apartment located at 2030 East 1st Street, East Westwick, Allstate 45678 (also their mailing address). They have lived in this apartment for the past four years. They last renewed their one-year lease on the 1st of the year. They own no real estate.

They own 2 vehicles, both of which have outstanding loans:

1992 Jeep Wrangler. $4,000 (value) purchased 3 years ago. It currently has 240,000 miles. The car is subject to a $4,559 security interest in favor of North Valley Credit Union (a/c # 3456). Monthly payments have been $450/month with 24 months remaining.

2000 Ford F150. $5,000 (value) purchased 3 years ago. It currently has 100,000 miles. The car is subject to a $5,985 security interest in favor of North Valley Credit Union (a/c # 4567). Monthly payments are $540 with 24 months remaining.

Henry owes ~$20,000 in past domestic support obligations (DSOs) (from another marriage). There is an existing wage garnishment order to the Department of Health and Human Services for the DSO obligation.

Both Henry and Martha owe past due income taxes (priority claims): $7,000 to the IRS, and $3,000 to the State taxing authority.

Henry works in construction, for Bermuda Contractors. Martha is currently unemployed. Henry's gross monthly income, before deductions for state and federal taxes, Social Security and Medicare is $3,440. His income has been steady and consistent for the past four years. Two years ago, before Martha became ill, her income was ~$40,000 per year. In the past two years, she has received ~$18,000 in unemployment income.

Monthly Deductions:

Payroll taxes and Social Security: $412;
Health and life insurance: $430;
Domestic Support Obligation wage order: $787.

Martha and Henry have been selling household possessions to financially survive over the past year. She expects to find employment soon. Here is a list of the Valencias' non-priority unsecured creditors:

Creditor	Amount of Non-Priority Unsecured Claim
• Allstate Bank	$ 4,000
• Binkley Bank (credit card)	$ 3,800
• Allstate Ambulance	$ 900
• DoorMart Club Visa (credit card)	$ 4,900
• Cap Two Bank (credit card)	$ 4,900
• Choose Bank (credit card)	$ 4,950
• Chest Medicine Associates	$ 3,000
• Ella Chaborne, M.D.	$ 950
• Allstate Medical Center	$ 94,000
• University Credit Union (credit card)	$ 3,800
• Neurosurgery Center	$ 13,500
• Radiology Associates	$ 9,500
• Southern Allstate Hospital	$ 2,500
• Spectrum Medical Group	$ 4,500
• 2nd Bank & Trust (credit card)	$ 3,500
TOTAL:	**$158,700**

Their monthly expenses are as follows:

Expense	Amount
• Rent	$1,200
• Food	$ 400
• Utilities (gas, electricity, phone, internet)	$ 360
• Clothing	$ 30
• Laundry/cleaning	$ 25
• Medical	$ 80
• Transportation (not including car payments)	$ 30
• Rental Insurance	$ 10
• Car Insurance	$ 73
TOTAL:	**$2,208**

You plan to charge the Valencias an $1,800 fee before filing. This amount includes attorney fees as well as the full bankruptcy filing fee.

In addition to the cars described above, the Valencias have the following assets:

Assets	Value
• Household goods, including furniture (no one item more than $400)	$ 1,500
• Books, CDs	$ 50
• Clothes	$ 1,000

• Wedding & engagement rings	$ 1,500
• Checking account #1	$ 50
• Checking account #2	$ 25
• Checking account #3	$ 25

You checked the relevant exemption statute (Allstate Statutes Annotated, §§ 101–106) and each of the above assets is exempt, to the full extent of its value.

Additional Information:

- The last four digits of their Social Security numbers:

Henry: 1234
Martha: 5678

- Both Martha and Henry plan to receive credit counseling this afternoon.
- Assumptions: Martha's maiden name was Rooth; they have no past business names.
- The Median Income in Allstate, according to Census data is $53,400.

After listening to your counsel and advice, they decide they want to file a joint petition under Chapter 13. The Trustee's statutory fee, as allowed by 28 U.S.C. § 586, is estimated to be 10% of the total plan payments. The Plan should build in $1,000 in additional legal fees.

Plan Goals:

- To save one vehicle by paying for it through the plan (the 1992 Jeep Wrangler — $450/month payment);

- To surrender the 2000 Ford F150 to North Valley Credit Union in full and final satisfaction of its claim;
- To continue paying DHHS through wage garnishment (since debtors can't afford to pay through the plan with Trustee commission);
- To pay Federal and State tax debt and a modest dividend to unsecured creditors.

Complete the Voluntary Petition, and relevant Schedules. Prepare a Chapter 13 Plan of Reorganization that meets the Bankruptcy Code's statutory requirements and achieves the Valencias' goals.

Questions and Things to Note:

1. Sections 1322 and 1325 describe the information required by the plan as well as the requirements for plan confirmation. Do you have enough information to formulate a Chapter 13 plan? Is there any information you still need to gather?

2. What is the applicable commitment period (meaning, how long must the plan last?) See § 1322(d)(1)?

3. The debtor must pay all projected disposable income (average monthly income earned during the 6 months before bankruptcy, minus necessary living expenses). How do you figure that out? Do you factor in Martha's unemployment income?

4. Note that not only do the Valencias have to sign the petition attesting as to its accuracy, YOU have to sign the petition as their attorney, attesting that the information in the petition and the schedules is correct. See §§ 342(b) and 707(b)(4)(D). What

kind of diligence should you do so that you can sleep at night (and keep your law license)?

The forms below can be downloaded at http://www.uscourts.gov/forms/bankruptcy-forms for use in conjunction with this exercise:

- Official Form 101–Voluntary Petition for Individuals Filing for Bankruptcy
- Official Form 106A/B–Schedule A/B: Property of the Estate
- Official Form 106C–Schedule C: The Property you Claim as Exempt
- Official Form 106D–Schedule D: Creditors Who Have Claims Secured by Property
- Official Form 106E/F–Schedule E/F: Creditors Who Have Unsecured Claims
- Official Form 106G–Schedule G: Executory Contracts and Unexpired Leases
- Official Form 106H–Schedule H: Your Co-debtors
- Official Form 106I–Schedule I: Your Income
- Official Form 106J–Schedule J: Your Expenses
- Official Form 122C-1–Chapter 13 Statement of Current Monthly Income and Calculation of Commitment Period

- Official Form 122C-2–Chapter 13 Calculation of Disposable Income

In addition, you can adapt the "Chapter 13 Plan" reproduced on the following pages for use in conjunction with this exercise. Similar or identical Chapter 13 Plans can be found with an internet search.

United States Bankruptcy Court
_________ District of ____________

In re: Case No: ____________

Debtor(s)

☐ Check if this is an amended plan

Official Form XXXX
Chapter 13 Plan

Date: ____________

Check all that apply:

- ☐ **The plan seeks to limit the amount of a secured claim, which may result in a creditor's lien receiving a partial payment or no payment at all, as set out in Part 2, Section 7.**
- ☐ **The plan requests the avoidance of a judicial lien as set out in Part 2, Section 9.**
- ☐ **The plan requests the avoidance of a nonpossessory, nonpurchase-money security interest as set out in Part 2, Section 10.**
- ☐ **The plan sets out non-standard provisions in Part 10.**

Notice to Interested Parties: Your rights may be affected. Your claim may be reduced, modified, or eliminated.

You should read these papers carefully and discuss them with your attorney, if you have one in this bankruptcy case. If you do not have an attorney, you may wish to consult one.

If you oppose the Plan treatment of your claim or any provision of this Plan, you or your lawyer must file an objection to confirmation at least seven days before the hearing on confirmation, unless otherwise ordered by the Bankruptcy Court. The Bankruptcy Court may confirm this plan without further notice if no objection to confirmation is filed. See Bankruptcy Rule 3015.

Part 1: Plan Payments and Length of Plan

1. Debtor(s) will pay to the trustee $_______ per month for ____ months, and

   $_______ per month for _____ months.

2. Payments to the trustee will be made from future earnings in the following manner:

   ☐ Debtor(s) will agree to entry of a payroll deduction order.

   ☐ Debtor(s) will make payments directly to the trustee.

3. Additional payments to the trustee will be made as follows (check all that apply):

❑ Debtor(s) will turn over to the trustee:

❑ any tax refunds received during the plan term

❑ any tax refunds in excess of $______ received during the plan term

❑ Other sources of funding, including the sale of property (describe source, amount and date when available):

____

4. The estimated total amount of plan payments is $ __________.

5. The estimated term of the plan is ______ months.

Part 2: Treatment of Secured Claims

6. **Cure of Default and Maintenance of Payments.** The debtor(s) will cure the default and maintain the contractual installment payments on the secured claims listed below. The allowed claim for the arrearage amount, if any, will be paid under the plan, with interest if specified, at the rate stated.

Name of creditor	Collateral	Current installment payment (including escrow payment)	Interest rate on arrearage (if applicable)	Amount of arrearage to be paid	Monthly plan payment on arrearage or other payment arrangement
		Payment: $________ Disbursed by: ❑ Trustee ❑ Debtor(s)			
		Payment: $________ Disbursed by: ❑ Trustee ❑ Debtor(s)			

7. **Determination of Allowed Secured Claims and Claim Modification.** The claims listed below are allowed secured claims only to the extent of the value of the creditor's interest in the collateral as provided under 11 U.S.C. § 506(a). Unless a creditor timely objects to confirmation, the value of the creditor's interest in the collateral shall be the amount of the allowed secured claim listed below, and it will be paid in full under the plan with interest at the rate stated below. The portion of any allowed claim that exceeds the amount of the allowed secured claim shall be treated as an unsecured claim under Part 4 of this plan. If the amount of a creditor's allowed secured claim is listed below as having no value, the creditor's allowed claim shall be treated in its entirety as an unsecured claim under Part 4 of this plan. The holder of any allowed secured claim, other than a mortgage treated in Part 2, Section 6, shall retain the lien until the earlier of (a) payment of the underlying debt determined under nonbankruptcy law, or (b) discharge under 11 U.S.C. § 1328(a), at which time the lien shall terminate and be released by the creditor. See Bankruptcy Rule 3015.

Name of creditor	Amount of creditor's claim	Collateral	Value of collateral	Amount of claims senior to creditor's claim	Interest rate	Amount of creditor's secured claim to be paid	Monthly plan payment

8. **Secured Claims Not Subject to 11 U.S.C. § 506.** The claims listed below were either (1) incurred within 910 days before the petition date and secured by a purchase money security interest in a motor vehicle acquired for the personal use of the debtor or (2) incurred within one year of the petition date and secured by a purchase money security interest in any other thing of value. These claims will be paid in full under the plan with interest at the rate stated below.

Check if applicable:

❑ Other secured claims not subject to 11 U.S.C. § 506 that are not listed below are provided for in Part 10 below.

Name of creditor	Collateral	Interest rate	Amount of claim to be paid	Monthly plan payment

9. **Judicial Lien Avoidance.** The judicial liens securing the claims listed below impair exemptions to which the debtor(s) would have been entitled under 11 U. S. C. § 522(b). A judicial lien securing a claim listed below shall be avoided to the extent that the lien impairs such exemptions upon entry of the order confirming the plan. The amount of the lien that is avoided will be treated as an unsecured claim in Part 4. The amount of the lien that is not avoided will be paid in full as a secured claim under the plan. See 11 U. S. C. § 522(f) and Bankruptcy Rule 4003(d).

Name of creditor	Collateral	Judgment date and date of lien recording	Lien recording inform-ation	Amount of lien not avoided and paid as secured claim	Interest rate (if applicable)	Monthly plan payment (if applicable)
				a. Amount of judicial lien $ ____ b. Amount of all other liens $ ____ c. Value of claimed exemptions + $ ____ d. Total. Add a, b, and c $ ____ e. Value of debtor's interest in property $ ____ Extent of exemption impairment (check applicable box): ❑ **Line d is greater than Line e.** The entire lien is avoided. ❑ **Line d is less than Line e.** A portion of the lien is avoided. Amount of lien not avoided: $ ____		
				a. Amount of judicial lien $ ____ b. Amount of all other liens $ ____ c. Value of claimed exemptions + $ ____ d. Total. Add a, b, and c $ ____ e. Value of debtor's interest in property $ ____ Extent of exemption impairment (check applicable box): ❑ **Line d is greater than Line e.** The entire lien is avoided. ❑ **Line d is less than Line e.** A portion of the lien is avoided. Amount of lien not avoided: $ ____		

10. **Nonpossessory, Nonpurchase-money Security Interest Avoidance.** The nonpossessory, nonpurchase-money security interests securing the claims listed below impair exemptions to which the debtor(s) would have been entitled under 11 U. S. C. § 522(b). A security interest securing a claim listed below shall be avoided to the extent that the security interest impairs such exemptions upon entry of the order confirming the plan. The amount of the security interest that is avoided will be treated as an unsecured claim in Part 4. The amount of the security interest that is not avoided will be paid in full as a secured claim under the plan. See 11 U. S. C. § 522(f) and Bankruptcy Rule 4003(d).

Name of creditor	Collateral	Amount of security interest not avoided and paid as secured claim	Interest rate (if applicable)	Monthly plan payment (if applicable)
		a. Amount of security interest $ ____ b. Amount of all other liens $ ____ c. Value of claimed exemptions + $ ____ d. Total. Add a, b, and c $ ____ e. Value of debtor's interest in property $ ____ Extent of exemption impairment (check applicable box): ❑ **Line d is greater than Line e.** The entire security interest is avoided. ❑ **Line d is less than Line e.** A portion of the security interest is avoided. Amount of security interest not avoided: $ ____		

		a. Amount of security interest $ ________ b. Amount of all other liens $ ________ c. Value of claimed exemptions + $ ________ d. Total. Add a, b, and c $ ________ e. Value of debtor's interest in property $ ________ Extent of exemption impairment (check applicable box): ❑ **Line d is greater than Line e.** The entire security interest is avoided. ❑ **Line d is less than Line e.** A portion of the security interest is avoided. Amount of security interest not avoided: $ ________		

11. **Surrender of Collateral.** The debtor(s) elect to surrender to the creditors listed below the personal or real property that is collateral for the claim. The debtor(s) consent to termination of the stay with respect to the collateral upon confirmation of the plan. Any allowed unsecured claim resulting from the disposition of the collateral will be treated in Part 4 below.

Name of creditor	Collateral

Part 3: Treatment of Administrative and Other Priority Claims

12. **Trustee's Fees.** Fees of the standing trustee will be paid in full, without interest. These fees are estimated to be ________% of plan payments; and during plan term, they are estimated to total $___________.

13. **Attorney's Fees.** Fees of the attorney, in the amount of $___________, will be paid in full, without interest.

14. **Other Priority Claims.** The allowed priority claims listed below will be paid in full.

Name of creditor	Basis for priority treatment	Amount to be paid

15. **Domestic Support Obligations Paid Less than Full Amount.** The allowed priority claims listed below based on a domestic support obligation will be paid less than the full amount of the claim in accordance with 11 U.S.C. § 1322(a)(4).

Name of creditor	Amount to be paid

16. **Interest.** Interest on allowed priority claims listed in line 15 will (check the applicable box):

❑ Not be paid

❑ Be paid at an annual percentage rate of _______ % in accordance with 11 U.S.C. § 1325(a)(4), and is estimated to total $ _______.

Part 4: Treatment of Nonpriority Unsecured Claims

17. **Cure of Default and Maintenance of Payments.** The debtor(s) will cure the default and maintain the contractual installment payments on the unsecured claims listed below on which the last payment is due after the final plan payment. The allowed claim for the arrearage amount will be paid under the plan.

Name of creditor	Current installment payment	Amount of arrearage to be paid
	Payment: $_______ Disbursed by: ❑ Trustee ❑ Debtor(s)	
	Payment: $_______ Disbursed by: ❑ Trustee ❑ Debtor(s)	

18. **Separately Classified Nonpriority Unsecured Claims.** The nonpriority unsecured allowed claims listed below are separately classified and will be treated as follows:

Name of creditor	Basis for separate classification	Treatment	Amount to be paid

19. **Nonpriority Unsecured Claims.** Nonpriority unsecured allowed claims that are not separately classified will be paid not less than (check the applicable box):

- ❑ The sum of $___________ to be distributed on a *pro rata* basis
- ❑ _______ percent of allowed claims
- ❑ The funds remaining after disbursements have been made to all other creditors provided for in this plan, to be distributed on a *pro rata* basis.

20. **Interest.** Interest on allowed unsecured claims, including separately classified claims, will (check the applicable box):

- ❑ Not be paid
- ❑ Be paid at an annual percentage rate of _______ % in accordance with 11 U.S.C. § 1325(a)(4), and is estimated to total $ _______.

Part 5: Executory Contracts and Unexpired Leases

21. All executory contracts and unexpired leases are rejected, except those listed below, which are assumed and will be treated as provided for below or under another specified provision of the plan.

Name of creditor	Property description	Treatment (refer to other plan section if applicable)	Current installment payment	Amount of arrearage to be paid
			Payment: $_______ Disbursed by: ❑ Trustee ❑ Debtor(s)	
			Payment: $_______ Disbursed by: ❑ Trustee ❑ Debtor(s)	

Part 6: Order of Distribution

22. The trustee will pay allowed claims in the following order:

1) ______________________
2) ______________________
3) ______________________
4) ______________________
5) ______________________
6) ______________________
7) ______________________

Part 7: Summary of Plan Disbursements

23. From the payments received from the debtor(s), the trustee will make the following estimated disbursements on allowed claims:

1) Current installment payments on secured claims (Part 2, Section 6 total): $ _______
2) Arrearage payments on secured claims (Part 2, Section 6 total): $ _______
3) Allowed secured claims (Part 2, Section 7 total): $ _______
4) Secured claims not subject to 11 U.S.C. § 506 (Part 2, Section 8 total): $ _______
5) Judicial liens not avoided (Part 2, Section 9 total): $ _______
6) Security interests not avoided (Part 2, Section 10 total): $ _______
7) Administrative and other priority claims (Part 3 total): $ _______
8) Current installment payments on unsecured debts (Part 4, Section 17 total): $ _______
9) Arrearage payments on unsecured debts (Part 4, Section 17 total): $ _______
10) Separately classified unsecured claims (Part 4, Section 18 total): $ _______
11) Nonpriority unsecured claims (Part 4, Section 19 total): $ _______
12) Interest on allowed unsecured claims (Part 4, Section 20 total): $ _______

13) Total of (1) through (12) above: $ _______

Part 8: Claims of Governmental Units

24. This plan is not binding with respect to any claim of a governmental unit that is (a) timely filed after confirmation of this plan, and (b) inconsistent with the treatment of such claim under this plan.

Part 9: Vesting of Property of the Estate

25. Property of the estate shall revest in the debtor(s) upon (check the applicable box):

- ❑ Plan confirmation
- ❑ Closing of case
- ❑ Other: ______________________________

Part 10: Non-standard Plan Provisions

In accordance with Bankruptcy Rule 3015(c), non-standard provisions are required to be set forth below.

Part 11: Signatures

Debtors (sign only if not represented by an attorney)

______________________ Date ______________

______________________ Date ______________

Debtors' Attorney

______________________ Date ______________

Time Sheet

DATE	CLIENT NAME	CLIENT BILLING NO.	DESCRIPTION OF WORK	TIME SPENT

CHAPTER 3

Property of the Estate and Disposable Income

- **SUBSTANTIVE PROBLEM/TOPIC:** Property of the Estate; Determining Disposable Income.
- **LEGAL RULES:** 11 U.S.C. §§ 541(a), 541(b)(7)(A), 707(b)(2)(A) & (B), 1306 and 1325(b)(2).
- **SKILLS:** Drafting a balanced advocacy piece.
- **STUDENT ASSIGNMENT:** Draft a memo and prepare for a hearing.
- **CLIENT BILLING NUMBER:** 204820.002

FACTS: Kayla and Donald Van Buren, both of whom are social workers, have been burdened by considerable credit card and medical debt since their only child was diagnosed with leukemia. They came to you to discuss the possibility of filing for bankruptcy. Both Kayla and Donald have been employed for over 12 years, and their income is above the state median. They are mindful of the need to plan for their future, so for the past 10 years they have been contributing a total of $318 per month to their respective 401(k) plans. In calculating their disposable income on Official Form 122C-2, they claimed a deduction of $318 per month for the voluntary 401(k) contributions on Line 41.

After running the means test, and discussing the issue with your clients, you determine that filing under Chapter 13 is their best option. You have prepared Debtors' Schedules I and J, which set out anticipated income and actual expenses, and the forms showed monthly net income of $5,559 and expenses of $4,672, for a monthly net income of $887. The plan you prepared proposes monthly payments of $569 for a term of 60 months, after deducting the $318 contribution into their 401(k) retirement accounts.

When you filed the Van Burens' plan on their behalf, the trustee objected, contending that their 401(k) contributions should not be allowed as an ongoing deduction in computing their disposable income. Next week is an evidentiary hearing before the judge, in which the court will consider the trustee's objection.

You know you will have an uphill battle making the argument that voluntary contributions to 401(k) retirement accounts should be included in debtors' disposable income, for purposes of calculating debt repayment through a Chapter 13 plan. You also know that the best way to prepare for the hearing is to identify and analyze all the arguments the trustee will make, as well as your best arguments for including the retirement contribution in the Van Burens' disposable income. Policy arguments are strong on both sides, but you also know that policy alone will not carry the day with your judge.

This issue has not been resolved in your jurisdiction. Write a comprehensive brief for the hearing, in which you analyze both side's strongest arguments.

Be prepared to make the argument on behalf of your client and think about the arguments the trustee will put forth and be prepared to address them.

Be sure to record your time for this project. You have already spent 12.5 hours meeting with the Van Burens, preparing their petition and schedules, running the means test, and responding to the trustee's requests for documents. Your current billing rate is $225/hour and the presumptive fee in your district is $3,500 for a Chapter 13 case.

Place to Start:

Read the discussion in your Casebook concerning the scope of property of the estate and how to calculate disposable income. You should also consider the following sources:

- 11 U.S.C. § 541, and specifically § 541(b)(7)(A).
- 11 U.S.C. §§ 1306, 1322(f) and § 1325(b)(2).
- *Lamie v. U.S. Trustee*, 540 U.S. 526, 534 (2004); *United States v. Ron Pair Enters., Inc.*, 489 U.S. 235, 241 (1989). Both cases stand for the proposition that questions of statutory interpretation begin with the plain language of the statute. If the statute is clear, the inquiry is at its end, and the statute should be enforced according to its terms.
- *Davis v. Mich. Dept. of Treasury*, 489 U.S. 803, 809 (1989) ("[S]tatutory language cannot be construed in a vacuum. It is a fundamental canon of statutory construction that the words of a statute must be read in their context and with a view to their place in the overall statutory scheme.")
- *Baxter v. Johnson* (In re Johnson), 346 B.R. 256, 263 (Bankr. S.D. Ga. 2006) (holding that § 541(b)(7) excludes all voluntary retirement contributions, both pre- and post-petition, from disposable income.)

- *In re Prigge*, 441 B.R. 667; *In re McCullers*, 451 B.R. 498, 503–05 (Bankr. N.D. Cal. 2011); *Seafort v. Burden* (In re Seafort), 669 F.3d 662, 673–74 (6th Cir. 2012) (holding that § 541(b)(7) does not permit exclusion of post-petition voluntary retirement contributions in any amount when determining disposable income).

- Section 401(k) retirement plans fall into the category of employee benefit plans described in § 541(b)(7)(A).

Time Sheet

DATE	CLIENT NAME	CLIENT BILLING NO.	DESCRIPTION OF WORK	TIME SPENT

CHAPTER 4

New in Town

- **SUBSTANTIVE PROBLEM/TOPIC:** Exemptions; Debtor moving from State to State
- **LEGAL RULES:** 11 U.S.C. § 522, Florida Homestead Exemption, Texas Homestead Exemption
- **SKILLS:** Statutory interpretation, legal analysis and client counseling (via e-mail).
- **STUDENT ASSIGNMENT:** Research and drafting an e-mail response to a prospective client's query.
- **PROFESSIONAL RESPONSIBILITY CONCEPTS:** Rule 1.1, attorney competence
- **CLIENT BILLING NUMBER:** 13579.001

FACTS: You are a newly licensed attorney working for, Bright & Caufield, a mid-sized law firm in beautiful Naples, Florida. You just received an e-mail from a prospective client, Stephanie Dillon. The email reads as follows:

> I moved to Florida last year from Austin, Texas. Before I left Texas, I sold my beautiful mid-century modern home on a ¼ acre lot in downtown Austin for $2.5 million dollars (clearing close to $1.8 million). When I moved to Naples, I used the proceeds of the sale of my Texas home to purchase for cash a small ocean-front bungalow (on a 1/16 acre lot) for $1.7 million. When I arrived in Florida, I started a great job as a management consultant. Things were going well until last month, when the CFO of my firm was caught

> embezzling $6.5 million, forcing the firm to liquidate and close. I am now unemployed, with few assets aside from my home and lots of accumulated debt (mostly credit card bills). Can I keep my house if I file for bankruptcy?

You know that both Texas and Florida have very generous homestead exemptions[1] and that the Bankruptcy Code says something about how to determine the applicable exemption statute when a debtor has recently moved between states. You also know that you have some research to do before responding.

Prepare a brief e-mail response to Ms. Dillon. Limit it to less than 200 words and be sure to avoid "legal jargon." You should also carefully consider the "tone" to strike: how formal or informal should you be?

While your firm provides "free" first time consultations for prospective clients, they require you to record your time for internal accounting purposes. Think about how much time you should record on your time sheet (time spent thinking about the issue, time spent reading the statutes, time on your first draft, time on a conversation with a colleague about the best approach to take).

Places to Start:

- Section 522 of the Bankruptcy Code
- Florida Constitution and Homestead Exemptions Statute
- Texas Homestead Exemption Statute

1 Florida and Texas exemption provisions are reproduced in Appendix C.

Time Sheet

DATE	CLIENT NAME	CLIENT BILLING NO.	DESCRIPTION OF WORK	TIME SPENT

CHAPTER 5

Relief from Stay

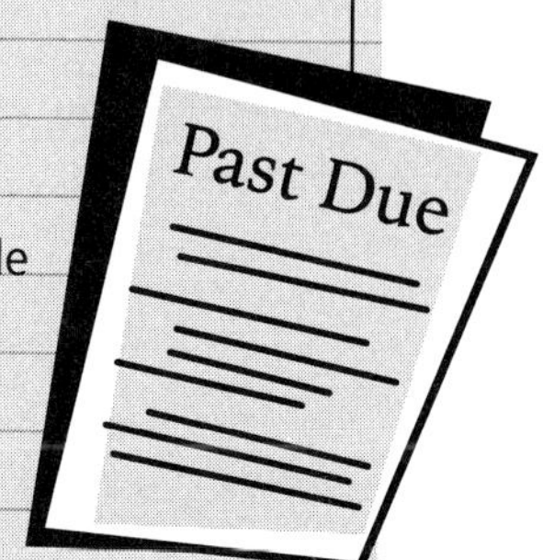

- **SUBSTANTIVE PROBLEM/TOPIC:** Determining a Client's eligibility for Relief from Stay

- **LEGAL RULES:** 11 U.S.C. § 362(a); Federal Bankruptcy Rule 4001; Federal Bankruptcy Rule 9014

- **SKILLS:** Statutory interpretation, legal analysis and drafting.

- **STUDENT ASSIGNMENT:** Determine whether your client is entitled to relief from stay, and if so, draft the motion (and other necessary documents) for filing.

- **CLIENT BILLING NUMBER:** 92746.001

FACTS: You are a new associate in a mid-sized firm that primarily represents creditors in bankruptcy matters. First Bank, a long-time client of the firm, holds a valid, duly perfected mortgage on Zachary and Tamara Dunbars' home. The mortgage, dated September 5, 2006, was filed in the office of the County Recorder in and for East County, Eastonia, on September 5, 2006, and recorded as Document No. 1206280. The mortgage covers the Dunbars' home, located in East County, Eastonia, legally described as follows: Lot eight (8), Block one (1) Plot two (2).

The Dunbars failed to make their mortgage payments from February 2014 through March 2015. They filed for Chapter 7 bankruptcy protection on April 2, 2015. At that time, the arrearage on their loan totaled $28,796.68, including late charges. The total mortgage debt is currently $384,995.28, including arrearages. Interest is currently accruing on the unpaid principal balance at $41.02 per day. The Dunbars' home has a current market value of $339,700.00. Zachary and Tamara have few other unencumbered assets.

First Bank does not want to wait the months it will take for the Chapter 7 case to be resolved; rather, it wants to foreclose on the property now. The Bank has asked you to take the steps necessary for it to do so. Determine whether First Bank is eligible for relief from the stay and if so, draft the motion. Also draft any and all documents that must be filed with the motion and indicate any necessary attachments.

Be sure to record your time for this work. Your current billing rate is $260/hour.

Points to Consider:

1. A motion is a written formal document in which a party requests the Bankruptcy Court to grant relief. The party requesting the relief, known as the Movant, must state the legal basis for the relief requested, and cite the applicable section(s) of the Bankruptcy Code and Bankruptcy Rules, and any relevant case law in the jurisdiction. A motion should be supported by all documents that support Movant's position. In this case, the standard for requesting relief from stay is whether Movant has a valid perfected security interest in the property, and whether the debtors have equity in the property.

2. A number of documents must be filed with the Motion for Relief from the Automatic Stay. Identify and draft them.

3. Is there a filing fee? If so, how much?

UNITED STATES BANKRUPTCY COURT
DISTRICT OF EASTONIA

In Re: Zachary Dunbar and Tamara Dunbar, Debtors

Chapter 7 Case
Case No. BKY 15-93881-ED.

MOTION FOR RELIEF FROM STAY

TO:

1.

2.

3.

4.

5.

6.

7.

8.

9.

WHEREFORE, Movant, by its undersigned attorney, moves the Court for an order modifying the automatic stay of 11 U.S.C. § 362(a) so as to permit Movant to foreclose its Mortgage on the Property and for such other relief as the Court may deem to be just, fair and equitable.

Dated this ___ day of April, 201X.

WATER & WELL, PC

BY:________________________________

UNITED STATES BANKRUPTCY COURT
DISTRICT OF EASTONIA

In Re: Zachary Dunbar and Tamara Dunbar, Debtors

Chapter 7 Case
Case No. BKY 15-93881-ED.

MEMORANDUM OF LAW

First Bank, (Movant) submits this memorandum of law in support of its motion for relief from the stay in the above-entitled matter.

FACTS

ARGUMENT

Dated this ___ day of April, 201X.

WATER & WELL, PC

BY:______________________________

Time Sheet

DATE	CLIENT NAME	CLIENT BILLING NO.	DESCRIPTION OF WORK	TIME SPENT

CHAPTER 6

Filing Together or Alone?

- **SUBSTANTIVE PROBLEM/TOPIC:** Chapter Choice (7, 11 or 13?); Filing a joint petition or filing as an individual; The consequences of not filing

- **LEGAL RULES:** Rules of Professional Responsibility 1.4 and 1.0(e); Bankruptcy Code §§ 707(b)(4), 524

- **SKILLS:** Document drafting & review

- **STUDENT ASSIGNMENT:** Drafting a letter to a client providing information and advice.

- **CLIENT BILLING NUMBER:** 37503.001

FACTS: You are a bankruptcy lawyer in a three-person firm, specializing in consumer and small business cases. Otto (age 37) and Darla (age 38) Cummings came in to your office yesterday for an initial consultation. Tearfully distraught, they told you the following story:

Otto and Darla have been married for twelve years, and have two small children, ages 5 and 7. Otto is a serial entrepreneur, most recently the sole shareholder in "The Studded Shirt," a company that manufactures and sells western clothing. Darla is a real estate broker with International Luxury Properties. After a number of years of prosperity and commensurate spending, they now find themselves over-indebted and hounded by creditors. The most tenacious of their creditors is the

Internal Revenue Service. Last month, Otto was forced to shut down his business and lay off all of his employees. All that remains of The Studded Shirt is debt, including $90,000 in payroll taxes incurred last year (his personal liability under the "control person" rule—also known as "hangover debt"). The Cummings also have $55,000 in credit card debt (some of it used to buy groceries, clothes for the kids, and other incidentals, and some of it used to cover operating expenses for Otto's business), $40,000 owed to a local bank (used for their most recent home improvement project), and $14,000 in medical bills (no health insurance until last year, and both kids were plagued with ear infections as babies). The Cummings' 5,500 square foot house overlooking the central valley was purchased with cash six years ago, when times were good. Darla, signing only a promissory note, also personally owes $20,000 to Buck Weatherbee, a state senator and loyal real estate client. Buck's loan was used to purchase her 2015 Audi A6 2.0T Premium, which Darla uses primarily to shuttle real estate buyers to house showings.

Otto and Darla have the following questions:

1. Is a bankruptcy filing the best option for them?

2. What are the real life implications of filing for bankruptcy? What will their post-bankruptcy life look like?

3. If bankruptcy is the best option, should they file jointly, or should just Otto file? If just Otto files, what will be the consequences for Darla?

4. They want to get on with their lives quickly, so Otto can start another business and Darla can sell more real estate. Can they file under Chapter 7?

5. For business and "political" reasons, Darla wants to repay Buck Weatherbee in full, either in or outside of the bankruptcy system. Can she do that?

Before the Cummings leave your office, they write a check for $1,500–your standard retainer fee. As you show them to the door, you reassure them that they will come out on the other side of this distressing situation, and you say brightly, "At least, you won't lose your home–you have that going for you." You also tell them that you have some issues to think about, but you will send them a letter, setting forth your thoughts by the end of the week.

Draft a letter to Otto and Darla Cummings, in which you explain:

1. Your professional responsibility to them as your clients;
2. What bankruptcy can and cannot do to help them;
3. If they decide to file, which chapter you recommend and why;
4. The relative pros and cons of a joint versus and individual filing;
5. Your specific recommendation as to their course of action, and why.

Points to Consider:

1. How will you explain your professional responsibility to the Cummings? Why should you?
2. How much can you rely upon the "story" presented by your clients? Should you do additional diligence? Can you afford to? Can you afford not to? Your billing rate is $260/hour.
3. Is this a business case or a consumer case? How do you make this determination? Once you decide, how much should you document your decision and decision-making process?
4. Your letter should be well organized, free of jargon, and offer a road-map enabling an informed decision.
5. You should keep track of (and be mindful) of time spent.
6. Attorneys in your state are governed by a set of rules identical to the ABA's Model Rules of Professional Conduct. Please consult these Model Rules on the ABA website, paying particular attention to the following rules: 1.0, 1.1, 1.2, 1.4, 1.5, 1.6, 1.7, 1.13, 1.14, 1.16, 2.1, 3.1, 3.3, 3.4, 4.1, 4.3, 5.1, 5.2, 5.4, 8.3, and 8.4.

Time Sheet

DATE	CLIENT NAME	CLIENT BILLING NO.	DESCRIPTION OF WORK	TIME SPENT

CHAPTER 7

Objecting to a Debtor's Discharge: Details Matter

- **SUBSTANTIVE PROBLEM/TOPIC:** Filing a Motion to Extend the Deadline for Objecting to a Debtor's Discharge

- **LEGAL RULES:** 11 USC §§ 523(a) & (c), 727; Federal Bankruptcy Rule 4007

- **SKILLS:** Document drafting and review

- **STUDENT ASSIGNMENT:** Review of an attorney's work product

FACTS: You are a new associate at Beezel & Cook, PC ("B & C"), which is known for representing clients in small business Chapter 11 cases. You have been with B & C for a week when Rogan, a senior partner, handed you a client file. In the file was a draft of a Motion to Extend the Deadline to Object to the Debtor's Discharge or Challenge the Dischargeability of Certain Debts (the "Motion"), prepared by a recently laid off second year lawyer, named Fester. Rumor has it that Fester was a rather lackadaisical associate, rushing through assignments and rarely proofreading his documents. He also had a sloppy habit of "cutting and pasting" paragraphs from other case documents without carefully reviewing his final work-product. Rogan asked you to review Fester's work, make any necessary edits, and get the Motion filed by the end of the business day. She was understandably concerned that the deadline to object to the debtor's discharge would pass without the client having a chance to determine whether there were grounds to object to debtor's discharge, or to the discharge of the debt owed. Rogan also reminded you to keep a careful record of your time.

The file reveals the following facts. Your client is Esther Pawley, the holder of a number of promissory notes signed by Burton Link, on behalf of Flibber, Inc. ("Flibber") (Client and Matter No: 63830.002). Link is the CEO of Flibber and has been under criminal investigation for self-dealing. Link personally filed for bankruptcy protection under Chapter 11 on January 9, 2016 in the Eastern District of Westerly. Link's case was converted to Chapter 7 on February 13, 2016 (Case No. 07-12-40164). Pursuant to the Order and Notice of the First Meeting (the "Order"), the first meeting of creditors (the "§ 341 meeting") was scheduled for March 8, 2016 and the deadline to object to Debtor's discharge or to challenge dischargeability of individual debts was set for May 7, 2016. On February 9, 2016, Link filed a Statement Concerning Debtor's Schedules and Statement of Financial Affairs (the "Statement") in which he disclosed that he is the subject of an ongoing criminal investigation and as such he would not answer any questions under oath and was asserting his Fifth Amendment privilege. He further stated that he would not file his bankruptcy schedules "unless and until he can be certain that they are true and complete." As of today, April 23, 2016, no schedules have been filed..

IN THE UNITED STATES BANKRUPTCY COURT FOR THE DISTRICT OF WESTERLY

IN RE: Chapter 11

Burton Link,
Debtor

Case No. 12–4164

MOTION TO EXTEND DEADLINE TO OBJECT TO DEBTORS' DISCHARGE OR CHALLENGE DISCHARBEABILITY OF CERTAIN DEBTS

COMES NOW Esther Pawly, bye and through her attorney of record, and moves this Court for an Order extending the deadline to object to Debtor's discharge or to challenge the dischargeability of certain debts, and as grounds shows unto the Court as follows:

Burton Fink originally filed for relief under chapter 11 of the Bankruptcy Code (the "Code") on January 9, 2012. His case was converted to a Chapter 7 on February 1, 2012.

Under the Order and Notice of the First Meeting, the First Meeting of Creditors pursuant to § 341 (the "Meeting") was scheduled for March 8, 2012. Under that same Order, the deadline to object to Debtor's discharge or to challenge dischargeability of certain debts is set for May 7, 2012.

On or about February 9, 2014, Debtor, through his attorney, filed a Statement Concerning Debtor's Schedules and Statement of Financial Affairs ("Statement"). In this Statement, Debtor disclosed that he is the subject of an ongoing criminal investigation and as such was asserting his Fifth Amendment privilege under the U.S. Constitution (the "Constitution"). He further stated that he would not file his Schedules "unless and until he can be certain that they are true and complete."

No Schedules have been filed. Debtor invoked his Fifth Amendment privilege at the First Meeting of Creditors.

Under Bankruptcy Rule 4001(d), any complaint to determine the dischargeability of a debt under 11 U.S.C. § 523(d) is to be filed no later than sixty (90) days after the first date set for the Meeting of Creditors under 11 U.S.C. § 341(a). Under that same Rule the Court may extend the time fixed for complaints to be filed to determine dischargeability of a debt. Presently, the time fixed (May 17, 2012) should be extended indefinitely until Debtor is in a position to file complete Schedules and Debtor is in a position to respond to questions at his First Meeting of Creditors or a 2040 Examination without having to invoke his Fifth Amendment privilege.

Esther Rawley holds certain promissory notes signed by Debtor, on behalf of Flibber, Inc. Pawley is investigating the facts and circumstances of the Debtor's self-dealing and commingling of corporate and individual funds. Debtor's action might very well lead to an action seeking that Debtor be found individually liable to Ms. Pawley and such liability be held non-dischargeable under 11 U.S.C. § 523(a)(8).

The guiding principles for summary judgment are well known. Summary judgment is proper where there is no genuine issue as to any material fact, and the moving party is entitled to judgment as a matter of law. *Celotex Corp. v. Catrett*, 477 U.S. 317, 322 (1986). The mere existence of some alleged factual dispute between the parties will not defeat an otherwise properly supported motion for summary judgment; the requirement is that there be no genuine issue of material fact. *Anderson v. Liberty Lobby, Inc.*, 477 U.S. 242, 247–48 (1986). In this case the dates for each material event are known to all parties, and are evident from the loan documents, land records and lien notices exchanged in discovery. Application of the federal statute to these material facts guides a disposition in favor of our client.

WHEREFORE, Esther Pawley respectfully requests this Court to indefinitely suspend the deadline date in which to file a complaint objecting to the discharge or the dischargeability of a certain debt until such time as

Debtor has filed all of his Schedules and can testify at his First Meeting of Creditors and/or a 2000 Examination without the necessity of invoking his Fifth Amendment privilege, and grant such other relief as is just.

DATED this the day of March, 201X.

Respectfully submitted /s/

Bar No. 704266

Time Sheet

DATE	CLIENT NAME	CLIENT BILLING NO.	DESCRIPTION OF WORK	TIME SPENT

CHAPTER 8

Can (Should) He File?

- **SUBSTANTIVE PROBLEM/TOPIC:** Chapter 7 vs. Chapter 13; Exempt property; Disposable income; Good faith; Discharge

- **LEGAL RULES:** 11 U.S.C. §§ 1325(a)(3), 1325(b)(2), 523(a)(6), 1328(a)(4) and 522(d)

- **SKILLS:** Drafting, statutory interpretation, legal analysis and client counseling

- **STUDENT ASSIGNMENT:** Drafting a memo to the file & client counseling

- **PROFESSIONAL RESPONSIBILITY CONCEPTS:** Can you (should you) represent someone who challenges the "good faith" bounds of the bankruptcy system?

- **CLIENT BILLING NUMBER:** 297458.001

FACTS: You are a junior associate at a law firm with an active bankruptcy practice. Mitchell Morath, who is a 62-year-old Maryland resident and financial advisor, met with your legal assistant last week, and you need to review his file notes in preparation for your meeting with Morath on Friday. The file notes reveal the following.

About five years ago, Morath's investment advisory firm, Morath Capital Partners, was floundering. In an effort to drum up additional business, Morath reincorporated under the name "Rockefeller Capital

Investors." More than once, he publicly and privately made reference to "my uncle Nelson." He, in fact, is not related to anyone named Rockefeller. Once he started implying a familial relationship with the Rockefeller family, business began rolling in.

About a year ago, Morath received a "cease and desist" order from a representative of the Rockefeller family, claiming that the Rockefeller family owns (and licenses to its affiliates) the common law rights and the registered trademarks for various "Rockefeller" marks. In light of the longstanding market presence of the Rockefeller family and its related entities, potential investors identify the registered "Rockefeller" marks with the financial services provided by the Rockefeller family and their companies. When Morath continued to operate his business under the name Rockefeller Capital Investors, the Rockefellers filed suit, alleging trademark infringement pursuant to 15 U.S.C. § 1114(1)(a), and other federal trademark claims pursuant to 15 U.S.C. §§ 1114 and 1125.

The district court granted, ex parte, an order authorizing expedited discovery and temporarily restraining Morath from "us[ing] the Rockefeller Capital, and any other Rockefeller-affiliated investment company names." After a hearing, at which Morath offered no defense or challenge, the district court converted the temporary restraining order into a preliminary injunction. When Morath failed to appear at trial and continued to solicit business under the Rockefeller name, the court entered a default judgment, announcing in open court that Morath acted intentionally, maliciously, and willfully when he used the Rockefeller name and trademarks to defraud investors. The court awarded the plaintiffs compensatory and punitive damages totaling approximately $160 million.

Morath now wants to file for bankruptcy. His scheduled assets are valued at $2,184,645, of which he claimed $2,140,501.25 to be exempt from the claims of his creditors. Of the assets claimed exempt, $1,413,888 is held in three individual retirement accounts.

Last month, Morath decided to close up his financial advisory shop and retire. As a result, his net monthly income decreased substantially from approximately $14,800 to approximately $2,650, which consisted primarily of monthly mandatory distributions from a state pension (acquired in a former job). Just before he shut his doors, he paid all his outstanding debts in full–except the trademark infringement judgment.

It is from the $2,650 that Morath proposes to make monthly payments of $750 to his remaining creditor. He told you he plans to support himself with his state pension, and with interest and dividends from exempt assets owned jointly with his wife.

Place to Start:

1. Prepare for your meeting by outlining the issues presented. Think through the kind of advice you can give him.

2. Be sure to record the time you spend preparing for this meeting. How many hours did you spend? What is this advice costing your client? Your current billing rate is $180/hour.

Issues to consider:

- Chapter 7 v. Chapter 13;
- Exempt property;
- Disposable income;
- Good faith;
- Discharge.

Sources to consider:

- 11 U.S.C. § 1325(a)(3)
- 11 U.S.C. § 1325(b)(2)
- 11 U.S.C. §§ 523(a)(6) & 1328(a)(4)
- 11 U.S.C. § 522(d)
- See 26 U.S.C. § 408(a)(6); 26 C.F.R. § 1.408–2(b)(6) (distributions from an IRA do not have to be taken until the taxpayer is age 70½).
- *In re Schnabel*, 153 B.R. 809 (Bankr.N.D.Ill.1993) ($6,000 lump-sum payment from retirement fund, which Chapter 13 debtor transferred into IRA, was asset of the estate rather than disposable income).
- Md.Cts. & Jud.Proc.Code Ann. § 11–504(g) (Maryland is an opt-out state for exemptions).
- Md.Cts. & Jud.Proc.Code Ann. § 11–504(h) (providing in relevant part, that "any money or other assets payable to a participant or beneficiary from, or any interest of any participant or beneficiary in, a retirement plan qualified under . . . Sec. 408 . . . of the United States Internal Revenue Code . . . shall be exempt from any and all claims of the creditors of the beneficiary or participant. . . ."). Morath's IRAs are qualified under 26 U.S.C. Sec. 408(a) and hence fall within the terms of the Maryland exemption.
- *Neufeld v. Freeman*, 794 F.2d 149 (4th Cir.1986) (announcing a totality-of-the-circumstances test for determining good faith,

taking in account factors such as: the percentage of proposed repayment to creditors, the debtor's financial situation, the period of time over which creditors will be paid, the debtor's employment history and prospects, the nature and amount of unsecured claims, the debtor's past bankruptcy filings, the debtor's honesty in representing the facts of the case, the nature of the debtor's pre-petition conduct that gave rise to the debts, whether the debts would be dischargeable in a Chapter 7 proceeding, and any other unusual or exceptional problems the debtor faces.)

3. *Velis v. Kardanis*, 949 F.2d 78, 82 (3d Cir.1991) ("Congress has expressed a deep and continuing interest in the preservation of pension plans, and in encouraging retirement savings, as reflected in the statutes which have given us ERISA, Keogh plans and IRAs.")

4. *Solomon v. Cosby* (In re Solomon), 67 F.3d 1128 (4th Cir. 1995).

5. *Patterson v. Shumate*, 504 U.S. 753, 764, 112 S.Ct. 2242, 2249–50, 119 L.Ed.2d 519 (1992).

Time Sheet

DATE	CLIENT NAME	CLIENT BILLING NO.	DESCRIPTION OF WORK	TIME SPENT

Reading Financial Statements (Not Beach Reading)

Financial Statement

There are a number of financial statements you will encounter in business bankruptcy practice. These include the balance sheet, income statement, and the cash flow statement. Each of these provides a valuable picture of the extent to which a business is financial healthy or in financial distress

The income statement, also known as the profit and loss statement, shows the financial performance of a firm over a period of time, typically monthly, quarterly or annually.

In contrast, the balance sheet shows the company's financial circumstances at a single date in time–a snapshot view. The balance sheet focuses on assets, liabilities and equity, as of a date certain, revealing what a company both owns and owes. Creditors are typically interested in borrowers' balance sheets, because they enable a creditor to determine whether the potential borrower has sufficient assets against which to borrow.

Company X Balance Sheet As of June 30, 201x	
Assets –	**Liabilities +**
Current Assets	Accounts Payable
Investments	Credit Card Balance

Property Plant and Equipment	Short-term Loans
Intangible Assets	Long-term Loans
TOTAL	**TOTAL**
	Equity

Individual clients (meaning people) are typically asked to produce personal financial statements. Personal financial statements are not balance sheets or income statements, but they include elements of both. This chapter will focus on describing the most common financial statements you will encounter when representing business clients.

What Goes in the Asset Column?

Assets are the things debtors own that have monetary value. For example, a business debtor may list assets including cash, inventory and property and equipment owned, as well as marketable securities (investments), prepaid expenses and money owed (accounts receivable) from customers. Assets also include valuable intangibles, like patents, trademarks and other intellectual property.

Assets are typically listed in categories or classes. The categories include:

- Current assets
- Investments
- Property, Plant & Equipment
- Intangible Assets

Or, assets can be categorized more simply, to include:

- Cash
- Equipment
- Inventory
- Accounts receivable

What are Liabilities?

Liabilities are debts owed to others. These may include, accrued wages, short-term credit, such as credit card debt and 60- or 90-day trade credit, as well as long-term loans owed to banks or other financiers.

Equity

Equity is the portion of the business assets owned by the shareholders. Equity is calculated by subtracting liabilities from assets–whatever is left over is the value of the owners' equity. If a company is "balance sheet" insolvent, liabilities exceed assets, and thus the shareholders' equity is zero.

This is not how you value a business, for purposes of a sale. Typically, the sales price of a business is based on a multiple of its earnings. Thus, the value of a business will usually (but not always) be greater than the owner's equity value (also called "book value").

The Balance Sheet Equation

The two sides of a balance sheet (assets and liabilities PLUS equity) ALWAYS add up to the same amount.

Let's use a simplified example. Assume that a sole proprietor, Miho Okahura, purchased a building worth $300,000 five years ago for her business. She made a down payment of 15% and took out a loan for the remainder of the balance.

Simplifying the example, and assuming the building is Ms. Okahura's only asset and the corresponding loan is her only liability, this is what her balance sheet looks like.

Miho Okahura Balance Sheet (in thousands) As of June 30, 200x	
Assets =	**Liabilities +**
Building $ 300,000	Long-term debt $255,000
TOTAL $300,000	**TOTAL $255,000**
	Equity $ 45,000

$300,000 (Assets) = $255,000 (Liabilities) + Equity ($45,000)

Assume that five years later, Ms. Okahura's building lost 10% of its value and that she has paid the loan down by $5,000. Her balance sheet should now look like this:

Miho Okahura Balance Sheet (in thousands) As of June 30, 200x + 5 years	
Assets =	**Liabilities +**
Building $ 270,000	Long-term debt $250,000
TOTAL $270,000	**TOTAL $250,000**
	Equity $ 20,000

Let's look at a slightly more complex example. Your client, Exdoc Media, Inc., has not been immune from the recession. Its cash on hand has been in serious decline, and it has had trouble paying its suppliers. Inventory has also declined in aggregate value, as some of its suppliers have refused to ship new inventory until Exdoc Media becomes current on its outstanding obligations to them.

Last year, Exdoc Media's balance sheet looked like this:

Exdoc Media, Inc. Balance Sheet (in thousands) As of June 30, 201x	
Assets =	**Liabilities +**
Cash $ 1,000	Accounts Payable (trade credit) $50,000
Inventory $ 70,000	Short-term Loans $ 30,000
Equipment $ 60,000	Long-term Loans $ 70,000
Accounts Receivable $35,000	Accrued Wages $300
TOTAL $166,000	**TOTAL $150,300**
	Equity $15,700

Today, Exdoc Media's Balance Sheet looks like this:

Exdoc Media, Inc. Balance Sheet (in thousands) As of June 30, 201x+ 1 year	
Assets =	**Liabilities +**
Cash $ 500	Accounts Payable (trade credit) $30,000
Inventory $ 40,000	Short-term Loans $ 35,000

Equipment $ 60,000	Long-term Loans $ 80,000
Accounts Receivable $20,000	Accrued Wages $300
TOTAL $125,000	**TOTAL $145,300**
	Equity ($20,300)

The Income or Profit & Loss Statement

The income statement, also known as the profit and loss statement, shows the financial performance of a person or a firm over a period of time—monthly, quarterly or annually. It calculates net income by subtracting total expenses from total income, and compares it to revenue and expenses from a prior period (year, quarter, month). When revenues and expenses are reported on the income statement for the period when cash is received and expenses incurred, this is known as cash-based accounting. When revenues and expenses are reported on the income statement when they are earned or incurred (typically before the cash is received and the expenses are paid), this is known as accrual-based accounting.

Exdoc Media **Income Statement** **Period ending December 31, 201X** **(thousands)**		
	201x	**201x–1**
Revenues		
Inventory Sales	20,000	45,000
Other Revenue	1,000	1,500
Expenses		
Cost of Sales	8,000	9,000
Operating Expenses	5,000	11,000
Other Expenses	4,000	2,500

Provision for Income Taxes	**2,000**	**4,000**
Income from Operations	21,000	46,500
Net Income	**2,000**	**20,000**

The income statement summarizes how the business incurs its revenues and expenses. It also shows the net profit or loss incurred over a specific accounting period. In this example, revenue from inventory sales has declined precipitously over the course of the year, with a commensurate decline in net income. Exdoc Media is showing all the signs of financial distress.

Cash Flow Statements

Finally, a bankruptcy lawyer must be able to understand at least the basics of a cash flow statement. A cash flow statement serves as a map that shows where cash came from and where it went. Being able to generate sufficient cash is key to maintaining a healthy business.

Simply put, a cash flow statement reports cash flow from operations. It shows how much cash the company started the given period with, how the company spent its cash, how the company received its cash, and the ending cash balance available for future investment or distribution to owners.

The three common classifications on Cash Flow Statements include operating activities, investing activities, and financing activities. Operating activities include the revenue-generating activities of a business entity—in other words, the cash from transactions undertaken by the business. Investing activities include assets held for investments (stocks, bonds), as well as the acquisition and sale of fixed assets such as equipment and real estate. Financing activities are those activities from which cash is derived. Financing can come from owners' equity and loans. Outflows can be payments on previous loans.

As set forth on the Annual Operating Cash Flow Statement set forth below, Exdoc Media is currently experiencing negative cash flow from operations.

Cash Flow Statement (in thousands)	June 30, 201X
Cash received from customers:	18,000
Cash paid to suppliers:	- 14,000
Cash paid to employees	- 7,000
Cash paid to landlords	- 2,300
Cash flows from operations:	- 5,300

Some things to keep in mind when reading financial statement: Balance sheets may not show the true, current value of assets. They typically value assets based on historical cost or on an estimated basis. Income statements also often include subjective judgments and estimates. Just because someone prepares a financial statement that looks like it was prepared correctly, that does not mean it accurately reflects a company's value.

Let's Test What You Have Learned

1. With respect to Exdoc Media's Operating Cash Flow Statement, what are some of the things you could advise, in order to help the business achieve a positive operational cash flow?

Let's try exercises with different facts:

2. Shawna Booth is a jewelry designer, operating as a sole proprietor. She operates her business out of a warehouse she owns, worth $160,000, encumbered by a $130,000 mortgage. She has a Toyota Prius, used to travel to jewelry and craft farts, worth $9,000, encumbered by a $6,000 security interest. Her workshop equipment assets are worth $10,000. She has $3,000 in her business bank account, $60 in her cash drawer, and owes a gem supplier $1,500.

Prepare Booth's balance sheet. What is she worth today?

Shawna Booth Balance Sheet **As of today**	
Assets =	**Liabilities +**
Cash $	Mortgage $
Real property $	Car Loan $
Equipment $	Other Loans $
Car $	
TOTAL $	**TOTAL $**
	Net worth/Equity $

3. Hotware Software Company currently has $50,000 in cash, and is obligor on a $45,000 unsecured loan. Its Balance Sheet currently reads:

Hotware Software Company Balance Sheet As of today	
Assets =	**Liabilities +**
Cash $ 50,000	Loan $45,000
Equipment $	
TOTAL $50,000	**TOTAL $45,000**
	Equity $ 5,000

Prepare balance sheets to reflect each of the following transactions.

a. Assume Hotware bought office equipment for $3,000 cash.

Hotware Software Company Balance Sheet As of today	
Assets =	**Liabilities +**
Cash $	Loan $
Equipment $	
TOTAL $	**TOTAL $**
	Equity $

b. Assume in the alternative that Hotware bought a company car on credit for $12,000.

Hotware Software Company Balance Sheet As of today	
Assets =	**Liabilities +**
Cash $ 50,000	Loan $45,000
Equipment $	Car Loan $
TOTAL $	**TOTAL $**
	Equity $

CHAPTER 10

A Business in Financial Distress: Reorganizing Furnishings Lab, Inc.

- **SUBSTANTIVE PROBLEM/TOPIC:** Reorganization under Chapter 11
- **LEGAL RULES:** Chapter 11 of the Bankruptcy Code and specifically 11 U.S.C. §§ 1101, 1115, 1121, 1122, 1123, 1124, and 11 U.S.C. §§ 327, 363, 364 & 365. Federal Rules of Bankruptcy Procedure 9003 & 9004
- **SKILLS:** Thinking through the information needed for a business to file a case under Chapter 11
- **STUDENT ASSIGNMENT:** Preparation of a pre-petition checklist of documents to gather and issues to think about in advance of filing Chapter 11 petition and schedules
- **PROFESSIONAL RESPONSIBILITY CONCEPTS:** Disclosure; Disinterestedness requirement for engagement of professionals
- **CLIENT BILLING NUMBER:** 4937503.004

FACTS: Furnishings Lab, Inc. (hereinafter, "Furnishings") is a privately held company, specializing in eclectic home furnishings, including furniture, artwork, lighting, tabletop items, textiles and decorative accessories from around the world. It also has a custom furniture business, taking orders through stores and its website, FurnishingsLab.com. Currently Furnishings has 57 stores in 18 states. Its stores are typically ~10,000 square feet and located in upscale malls or lifestyle centers.

Over the past three years, Furnishings has faced a significant slump in sales, largely attributable to a general softness in the economy. It has also been adversely affected by competitors' "mark-down fever." As a seller of high-end home decor items, Furnishings' troubles are not an anomaly. As financially stretched consumers focus more on basic necessities, they have been spending less on discretionary items.

The drop in sales has forced Furnishings to close 6 of its stores over the past 24 months (fortunately, the leases were expiring just as these stores were closed). The decline in sales accelerated over the past year and has continued, unabated, into the first quarter of this year.

In a recent press release, Cara Thompson, co-founder and chief financial officer, announced Furnishings' plan to file for Chapter 11 bankruptcy. "In light of current economic conditions, our company has had to make some difficult decisions," she said. Citing "severe" sales decline as the primary issue driving its bankruptcy, Thompson pledged that Furnishings would emerge from bankruptcy as a reorganized and reinvigorated business.

Furnishings has sufficient cash to continue operating its business. Thompson noted it plans to unload leases from an additional 15 stores. These stores are either underperforming or in markets the company decided it would no longer serve.

Your firm has been hired by Furnishings as bankruptcy counsel. Senior Parter Bogon has asked you to start gearing up for the case.

Review the Official Forms specified below (which are available on the U.S. Courts website). Prepare a pre-petition checklist of all of the documents needed in order to prepare the Petition and Schedules.

What are some of the issues with respect to the debtor's continuing operations that you need to start thinking about? Key suppliers? Key employees? Relationships with existing lenders?

As always, be sure to record the time you spend on this assignment.

The forms below can be downloaded at
http://www.uscourts.gov/forms/bankruptcy-forms
for use in conjunction with this exercise:

- Chapter 11 Voluntary Petition for Non-Individuals [Form 201]
- Attachment to Voluntary Petition [Form 416B]
- Official Form 204–List of 20 largest creditors
- Chapter 11 Schedules
  Form 206A/B
  Form 206D
  Form 206E/F
  Form 206G
  Form 206H
  Form 206 Sum

Time Sheet

DATE	CLIENT NAME	CLIENT BILLING NO.	DESCRIPTION OF WORK	TIME SPENT

CHAPTER 11

Operational First Day Motions: Payment of Furnishings Lab's Pre-Petition Employee Wages and Benefits

- **SUBSTANTIVE PROBLEM/TOPIC:** First Day Motions: Motion to use Cash Collateral
- **LEGAL RULES:** 11 U.S.C. §§ 105, 327, 363, 364(b), 507(a)(4), 507(a)(5), and 541(d)
- **SKILLS:** Drafting an Operational First Day Motion
- **STUDENT ASSIGNMENT:** Drafting
- **CLIENT BILLING NUMBER:** 6387322.004

FACTS: After the flurry of filing the Petition and Schedules, it is now time to turn attention to the smooth continuation of business operations, such as being able to continue to manage cash, get shipments of inventory and supplies from critical vendors, pay sales and use taxes, keep the lights on, and pay pre-petition employee wages and benefits. Furnishings Lab, as debtor-in-possession of the estate, must petition the court to take certain actions.

You found an Employee Wage and Benefits Motion of another retail bankruptcy: Harry and David (a copy of this motion is available at www.developingprofessionalskills.com). Using this as an example, you should draft a motion on behalf of Furnishings asking for court permission to pay the pre-petition wage and benefit claims of necessary employees, incurred in the ordinary course of business. After doing some research, you discover that Furnishings Labs pays it employees at the end of each month during which the employee worked. Furnishings also provides its full-time employees with medical, dental, vision, life and disability insurance, as well as 7 days sick time and 3 personal days. It also makes matching contributions to 401(k) and 403(b) savings plans.

An employee wage and benefits motion should categorize and specifically describe each category of the employee benefits subject to the motion. Unless otherwise justified under the doctrine of necessity, an employee wage and benefits motion should also note that the debtor-in-possession intends to pay all wages and benefits in accordance with the priority arrangement set forth in by 11 U.S.C. §§ 507(a)(4) and (5).

Time Sheet

DATE	CLIENT NAME	CLIENT BILLING NO.	DESCRIPTION OF WORK	TIME SPENT

CHAPTER 12

Substantive First Day Motions: Furnishings Lab's Retail Lease Rejection

- **SUBSTANTIVE PROBLEM/TOPIC:** Rejection of retail leases
- **LEGAL RULES:** 11 U.S.C. § 365; F.R.B.P. 6006
- **SKILLS:** Drafting a First Day Motion
- **STUDENT ASSIGNMENT:** Drafting
- **CLIENT BILLING NUMBER:** 6387322.004

FACTS: Once Fine Furnishings has filed its petition and schedules, it must continue its ordinary course of business operations. It must however, petition the bankruptcy court for approval of major business decisions. These include:

- sales of assets, such as property or real property, out-of-the-ordinary course of business;
- entering into or getting out of (rejecting) leases of real or personal property;
- post-petition secured lending transactions (real or personal property);
- shutting down or expanding business operations;

- entering into or modifying contracts and agreements, other than in the ordinary course of business; and

- retention of, and payment of fees and expenses to, attorneys and other professionals.

The bankruptcy court will consider input from creditors and other parties in deciding whether to approve out-of-the ordinary course of business actions, but formal votes by creditors and equity holders are taken only in connection with proposed Chapter 11 plans.

Prior to the case filing, Furnishings' CFO Cara Thompson assessed the profitability of each of Furnishings' store locations. Thompson has determined that Furnishings could not continue to operate outside of the protection of a Chapter 11 case and needs to immediately close 15 operating locations and reject each of these leases. Further, in the event that Furnishings must close additional stores, it needs to be able to react quickly to immediately reject other store leases in order to preserve the estate for the benefit of its creditors.

Based upon her knowledge of the current real estate market for retail space and upon the advice of professionals, Thompson believes that the 15 store leases are no value to the estate. If Furnishings were required to keep these leases and perform under them while it marketed and attempted to assign them, the administrative expenses would be prohibitive in light of the fact that the closed lease locations are not generating any income. The aggregate monthly rent and other charges under these Leases is approximately $550,000, which will be an administrative expense of the estate if the leases are not rejected immediately. Thus, Thompson has determined that immediate rejection of the 15 leases is in the best interest of the estate.

Thompson notified the affected landlords and vacated, surrendering the keys to these properties, prior to the petition date. Thus, there will be no element of surprise in the immediate rejection of the closed store leases.

You have been asked to draft an Emergency Motion for Order Establishing a Procedure for the Future Rejection of Non-Residential Real Property Leases and the Abandonment of Personal Property and Authorizing the Rejection of Non-Residential Real Property Leases and the Abandonment of Certain Personal Property. Review the Motion filed on behalf of another retail bankruptcy debtor-in-possession, and draft an outline of the Motion to be filed on behalf of Furnishings.

A copy of this motion is available at:
www.developingprofessionalskills.com

Time Sheet

DATE	CLIENT NAME	CLIENT BILLING NO.	DESCRIPTION OF WORK	TIME SPENT

Appendix A

Reprinted with Permission from the American Bankruptcy Institute

Competency for Debtors' Counsel

Introduction[2]

Rule 1.1 of the MODEL RULES OF PROFESSIONAL CONDUCT, adopted by most states and the District of Columbia, sets forth the standard for lawyer competency: "A lawyer shall provide competent representation to a client. Competent representation requires the legal knowledge, skill, thoroughness and preparation reasonably necessary for the representation."[3] Comment 5 to Model Rule 1.1 states that "[c]ompetent handling of a particular matter includes inquiry into and analysis of the factual and legal elements of the problem, and use of methods and procedures meeting the standards of competent practitioners." In addition to the standard set forth in Rule 1.1, most federal courts, including some bankruptcy courts, have adopted a court-specific competency standard.[4] These standards typically include the requirement that lawyers are familiar with the applicable rules of procedure, evidence, and in some cases, substantive law.

The generalized pronouncement that a lawyer must be "competent," however, does not provide specific needed guidance to lawyers, clients,

2 Reporters Nancy B. Rapoport and Lois R. Lupica would like to thank Task Force members Richard P. Carmody, James H. Cossitt, Steven A. Schwaber, and Andy Vara for their excellent background research that formed the basis of this Report.

3 MODEL RULE OF PROFESSIONAL CONDUCT R. 1.1.

4 S.D. Cal. Civ. Local R. (2011), *available at* http://www.casd.uscourts.gov/uploads/Rules/Local%20Rules/LocalRules.pdf; Ariz. Bankr. L. R., *available at* http://www.azb.uscourts.gov/default.aspx?PID=16 (last visited Aug. 3, 2012).

or judges about what precise skill sets a lawyer must have in order for him or her to provide competent client representation. As such, this Report describes, with some specificity, the substantive information that a bankruptcy lawyer must understand, as well as some of the specific skills that the lawyer must possess, to provide competent representation to a debtor in bankruptcy.

The Bankruptcy Context

Bankruptcy is a complex area of law, practiced in myriad contexts, with very different types of debtors accessing the bankruptcy system. For example, the bankruptcy reorganizations of public companies such as General Motors and American Airlines implicate very different issues and require different sets of skills for debtors' lawyers than the liquidation of small privately-held business enterprises. Further, the representation of a consumer debtor in a Chapter 13 case requires a body of knowledge and strategy significantly different from that required to represent, for instance, a liquidating nursing home.

Because the context and type of client can be so varied across the spectrum of potential debtors, bankruptcy lawyers typically specialize. They usually restrict their practice to consumer bankruptcy or business bankruptcy cases.[5] Lawyers within the two broadest bankruptcy categories may further specialize: some attorneys may primarily represent Chapter 13 debtors, while others may primarily represent

5 Although it is not unusual for lawyers to represent both consumers and small businesses, including sole proprietors (and in fact, there are lawyers with dual certifications as specialists in business and consumer bankruptcy law), it is less typical for lawyers to represent consumers and large business debtors in complex reorganizations or liquidations. *See* Lois R. Lupica, *The Consumer Bankruptcy Fee Study: Final Report*, 20 Am. Bankr. Inst. L. Rev. 17, 93 (2012). Even if a lawyer typically represents a particular type of debtor or files most of his or her cases under one chapter or category (*e.g.*, chapter 13 and consumer chapter 7 cases), the competency standard requires that the lawyer be able to recognize a range of bankruptcy-related issues that may arise in individual cases, as well as the circumstances when a client may benefit from relief under another chapter.

debtors who file under Chapter 7; yet others may focus on the representation of sole proprietors and small family businesses or individual Chapter 11 reorganizations. Business bankruptcy lawyers may develop a specialization by the type of debtor, using such categories as market capitalization or industry sector. A lawyer must recognize the extent to which each of these individual types of bankruptcy practices requires different bodies of knowledge and skill sets. As noted below, to the extent that the lawyer's client or the type of case implicates issues about which the lawyer has little or no knowledge or with which he has little or no experience, the lawyer should either seek to educate himself (time and resources permitting) or seek counsel or assistance from a professional with experience and expertise in the particular issue or matter.[6]

Although the objective of this Report is to list the core competencies and skills required to represent both consumer and business debtors competently, the Task Force is mindful that many, if not all, of these same competencies and skills are required to represent the other parties in interest in bankruptcy cases. Some of these parties include trustees, examiners, ombudsmen, secured and unsecured creditors, various official and ad hoc committees, indenture trustees, lenders, asset purchasers and brokers, liquidators, landlords, trade suppliers, franchisers and franchisees, licensors and licensees, and equity owners. The representation of these parties will require lawyers to have similarly specialized skills and knowledge, tailored to their

6 *See* Model Rule 1.1 cmt. 2 and Model Rule 1.2 cmt. 6.

clients' role in the bankruptcy process, in order to provide competent representation to their clients.[7]

The Task Force's primary goal is to ensure that debtors receive the competent representation to which they are entitled. Although this Report detailing "best practices" for bankruptcy lawyers is not seeking to restrict entry into bankruptcy practice, the Report recognizes that bankruptcy practice is complex and specialized and demands a substantial investment of time in the form of education and practical experience over a career. There is no lack of reasonably-priced educational resources available to aspiring bankruptcy lawyers. Lawyers for all parties in a bankruptcy proceeding or case also should realize that there are significant risks in providing less than competent representation, such as being subject to fee reductions, sanctions, civil liability and, in rare instances, criminal liability.

Consumer Practice

Consumer debtors, according to the Bankruptcy Code's definition, are individuals who have incurred debts primarily for personal, family, or household purposes.[8] The vast majority of consumer bankruptcy filers

7 The focus of the discussion in this proposal is on counsel for the debtors in consumer and business bankruptcy cases. Similar capacities, skill sets, and competencies are necessary for counsel for other participants in the bankruptcy process (*e.g.*, counsel for creditors, counsel for a standing, panel, or case trustee, and committee counsel), albeit in a somewhat different context. A thorough discussion of specific best practices for counsel for parties other than the debtor in bankruptcy is outside of the scope of this Report. We recognize that competency is not solely an issue with respect to debtors' counsel, but with the debtor's fresh start on the line, competent representation through the bankruptcy process is an 'all or nothing' event for debtors. For this and a variety of other reasons, including time and resource issues, the Task Force chose to focus on the issue of competency of counsel in this one role. Other ABI working groups may choose to pursue competency issues of counsel serving in other roles.

8 11 U.S.C. § 101(8). Many individual debtors, however, file for bankruptcy seeking to discharge business debts. The debtor typically incurs these business debts in the course of operating a small business.

are represented by counsel.[9] Because there are numerous complex legal and strategic decisions to be made in even in the simplest no- or low-asset consumer case, competent counsel serves as a valuable guide through the bankruptcy labyrinth. If a consumer client in financial distress presents a more complicated scenario, such as wanting to retain a home or car by paying the debt over time, then the need for legal advice from a knowledgeable attorney becomes even more compelling.[10] The absence of professional counsel can adversely affect both seemingly simple and complex consumer bankruptcy case outcomes, as well as the long-term value of the remedy of bankruptcy.[11]

A lawyer seeking to represent a consumer debtor must possess certain core competencies and skills.[12] These include an awareness of alternatives to the bankruptcy system, an understanding of bankruptcy as a substantive and procedural remedy, knowledge of the bankruptcy process, the skill to provide counseling to a client in financial and emotional distress, proficiency in the courtroom, the ability to negotiate with multiple parties with adverse interests, the judgment to aid a client to make decisions in his or her best interest, and the diligence

9 In most jurisdictions, a small percentage of consumers file for bankruptcy *pro se*. Lupica, *supra* note 6, at 139. In some jurisdictions, however, the percentage of *pro se* cases is considerably higher than the national mean. *See e.g., In re Castorena*, 270 B.R. 504, 524–26 (Bankr. D. Idaho, 2001)("... fully 90% of the debtors filing in this District [retains] ... a licensed lawyer to assist them in successfully navigating the statutory channels of bankruptcy law.")

10 A recent empirical study of thousands of randomly selected consumer bankruptcy cases found that no *pro se* Chapter 13 debtors received a discharge. Lupica, *supra* note 6, at 81.

11 "The counseling of a client in financial matters, particularly about his or her choice of remedies under the Bankruptcy Code or whether a bankruptcy proceeding can be avoided, is a serious matter that deserves the attention of a qualified attorney." *Columbus B. Ass'n v. Flanagan*, 77 Ohio St. 3d 381, 383, 674 N.E.2d 681, 683 (Ohio 1997).

12 This section addresses primarily representation of consumers under chapter 13 and chapter 7. Individual Chapter 11 cases are a hybrid between Chapter 11 business reorganization and Chapter 13 cases. If individuals want or need to reorganize their finances, and they exceed Chapter 13 debt limits, Chapter 11 offers an option. The process of representing an individual under Chapter 11 is considerably different than representing a debtor under Chapter 7 or 13, but there are similarities in the general skills required of an attorney.

to see what can be an arduous process through to its resolution. By agreeing to represent a consumer bankruptcy debtor, a lawyer is certifying that he or she possesses the requisite legal knowledge and skills. Further, the lawyer accepts the trust and reliance of his or her client to provide competent representation in response to the client's oft-changing needs.

The core capacities and skills possessed by a competent lawyer representing consumer bankruptcy debtors include, but are not limited to, the following:

1. A lawyer should understand and be able to communicate to his or her client the advantages and disadvantages of bankruptcy as a debt relief remedy.

Comment: At the first client meeting, prior to any bankruptcy filing, the lawyer should be able to evaluate whether bankruptcy is the appropriate remedy for the particular consumer's problems.[13] As a "debt relief agency" under the Bankruptcy Code,[14] the lawyer must be able to assess the particular facts and circumstances presented by the client in order to weigh them against the advantages and disadvantages of filing a bankruptcy case. If the lawyer and client conclude that bankruptcy is an appropriate remedy, the lawyer's next concern is the appropriate chapter under which to file and the proper timing

13 *See In re* Pereira Santiago, 457 B.R. 172, 176 (Bankr. D.P.R. 2011) (citing 9 William L. Norton Jr., Bankr. L. & Prac. 3d § 172.25) ("Attorneys must explain the benefits, burdens, and consequences of bankruptcy to their clients to the extent reasonably necessary to permit informed decisions about the case."); *In re* DeSantis, 395 B.R. 162, 169 (Bankr. M.D. Fla. 2008) ("Attorneys must explain the rules and assist debtors in making good decisions.").

14 *See* 11 U.S.C. § 101 (12A) ("The term 'debt relief agency' means any person who provides any bankruptcy assistance to an assisted person in return for the payment of money or other valuable consideration, or who is a bankruptcy petition preparer under section 110, but does not include [certain exceptions]"). Under 11 U.S.C. § 101(3), ('[t]he term 'assisted person' means any person whose debts consist primarily of consumer debts and the value of whose nonexempt property is less than $150,000.").

for filing. The timing consideration requires the lawyer to understand the consequences of a decision to file now in order to address exigent issues (such as a pending foreclosure sale or an eviction proceeding), or to wait in order to engage in acceptable pre-bankruptcy planning.

Pre-bankruptcy planning requires the identification of applicable and available exemptions, a discussion of tax liabilities, and the identification of any pre-petition financial transactions, to name a few. A review of the consumer's eligibility for relief under each chapter includes a consideration of any prior cases filed, the constraint imposed by statutory debt limits, and the balance between the debtor's consumer and non-consumer debts, as well as an appraisal of the benefits, burdens, and intended and unintended consequences offered by each chapter.

2. A lawyer should be familiar with the information necessary to prepare a bankruptcy case. In addition, the lawyer must have developed efficient and effective systems and procedures to obtain from the client the information and documentation required by the Bankruptcy Code.

Comment: Before a bankruptcy case is filed, a lawyer representing a consumer debtor must recognize the need to assemble and evaluate accurate and complete information and documentation from his or her client. This information and documentation should include copies of (a) pay advices; (b) tax returns; (c) bank statements; (d) inventories of all property owned by the debtor; (e) itemizations of all debts owed by the client, with appropriate back-up documentation; (f) itemizations of real estate owned and mortgages obligated on with appropriate back-up documentation; (g) financial statements and other financial information necessary to complete required schedules; (h) itemizations of all expenses in appropriate detail; and (i) a credit report. This list is not exhaustive, and the lawyer should be mindful of any additional information necessitated by the facts of a particular case.

In addition, the lawyer must be aware of the dictates and prohibitions set forth in the governing state rules of professional conduct on criminal or fraudulent behavior, including engaging in criminal, fraudulent, or prohibited transactions.[15] The lawyer must further be familiar with the evolving case law relating to pre-bankruptcy and exemption planning, including the line between permissible and impermissible conduct. It is the responsibility of the lawyer to apply the relevant rules to his or her client's goals and advise the client as to whether the proposed conduct is clearly proper, clearly improper, or falls within the gray area between the two ends of the spectrum. If the proposed conduct falls in the gray area, the lawyer must provide appropriate guidance and an informed opinion sufficient to allow the client to make an informed decision. The lawyer must make reasonable inquiry to ensure information supplied by the consumer debtor is accurate and complete. The scope of the reasonable inquiry to be performed by debtor's counsel may vary depending upon the type of client, the size of the case and the scope of the issues presented.[16]

3. A lawyer should be aware of the Bankruptcy Code provisions mandating certain disclosures by the lawyer. A lawyer should also know what types of information he or she is required to communicate to consumer debtor clients.

Comment: The Bankruptcy Abuse Prevention and Consumer Protection Act of 2005 (BAPCPA) requires attorneys to make certain disclosures and provide specific information to their consumer debtor clients. A lawyer should know that each of the following should be provided to his or her client: (i) a form notice under 11 U.S.C. § 342(b) and § 527(a)(2) describing bankruptcy's requirements and consequences,

15 Model Rules of Professional Conduct R. 1.2(d) prohibits a lawyer from "counseling a client to engage, or assist a client in conduct that the lawyer knows is criminal or fraudulent . . . ." Official Comments 9, 10, and 12 offer lawyers further guidance.

16 *See, e.g.*, Task Force on Att'y Discipline Best Practices Working Grp., Ad Hoc et. al., *Working Paper: Best Practices for Debtors' Attorneys*, 64 Bus. Law. 79, 82 (2008).

(ii) general information about legal services and rights of an assisted person, (iii) a form notice setting forth general information on how to arrive at certain values and information mandated by the official schedules, statements and forms, and (iv) a fully executed written contract (a retention letter) that identifies the services to be provided and the fees or charges for such services.[17]

In addition, the lawyer should facilitate the client's enrollment in the credit counseling course required of all consumer debtors as a predicate to filing a petition.[18]

4. A lawyer should know how to efficiently and effectively prepare and file a bankruptcy petition and the related schedules, statements and other necessary documents.

17 *Id.; see also* Ad Hoc Comm. on Bankr. Ct. Structure and Insolvency Processes, & Task Force on Att'y Discipline, ABA Section of Bus. Law, *Attorney Liability Under Section 707(b)(4) of the Bankruptcy Abuse Prevention and Consumer Protection Act of 2005*, 61 Bus. Law. 697, 717 (2006). If the scope of the representation is limited, the specific services to be provided should be explicitly described. *See* ABI Task Force on National Ethics Standards Report on Best Practices for Limited Services Representation in Consumer Bankruptcy Cases (April 2013); H. Slayton Dabney, Jr., Stefanie Birbrower Greer, Richelle Kalnit & Daniel G. Egan, *Retention and Payment: Essentials of Being Retained and Paid as Debtor's Counsel in Chapter 11* (2008).

18 The debtor in a Chapter 7 "asset" case was deemed to have satisfied the Bankruptcy Code's credit counseling requirement without filing his credit counseling certificate; debtor had stated under oath that he had completed the credit counseling required by the BAPCPA and would file his credit counseling certificate, debtor later failed to file the certificate. When debtor later failed to file the certificate and to appear at the first meeting of creditors, the debtor was found to be judicially estopped from denying that he completed the requisite credit counseling. Robin Miller, *Validity, Construction, and Application of Credit Counseling Requirement Under Bankruptcy Abuse Prevention and Consumer Protection Act (BAPCPA), 11 U.S.C.A. § 109(h)*, 11 A.L.R. Fed. 2d 43 (originally published in 2006); *see also* Lindsay Sherp, *To Strike or To Dismiss, That Is the Question. How Courts Should Dispose of Bankruptcy Cases Filed by Debtors Who Failed to Obtain Credit Counseling*, 60 Baylor L. Rev. 317, 320 (2008) ("By requiring individual debtors to undergo credit counseling before filing for bankruptcy, Congress 'intended to give consumers in financial distress an opportunity to learn about the consequences of bankruptcy—such as the potentially devastating effect it can have on their credit rating—before they decide to file for bankruptcy relief.' In other words, Congress has determined that bankruptcy should be a last resort instead of 'the first place where an individual consumer debtor turns for help.'").

Comment: Once a lawyer has conducted his or her initial client counseling, gathered the necessary information and documentation, made the required disclosures, and provided advice with respect to the appropriate case, the lawyer must then prepare the necessary petition, schedules, statements, and forms. Preparation of these documents requires the lawyer to know how to analyze the available and applicable exemptions, determine the appropriate treatment of collateralized debts, (e.g., surrender, redemption, reaffirmation, or retention), evaluate priority debts and administrative claims, and assess the debtor's ability to repay creditors from income or assets. If the debtor is filing a case under Chapter 13, the lawyer must also prepare the Chapter 13 plan.[19]

As noted above, the lawyer must make reasonable inquiry to ensure information supplied by the consumer debtor is accurate and complete and must conduct an inquiry sufficient to satisfy his or her obligation to sign the petition pursuant to Section 707(b)(4)(D) of the Bankruptcy Code.[20] As recently observed, "[w]here a lawyer systematically fails to take any responsibility for seeking adequate information from her client, makes representations without any factual basis because they are included in a "form pleading" she has been trained to fill out, and ignores obvious indications that her information may be incorrect, she

19 If the debtor is not eligible for chapter 7 and has debts that exceed the chapter 13 debt limits, an individual chapter 11 case may be appropriate. In such instance, the lawyer for the debtor must be aware of the host of specific issues that arise in such cases. *See, e.g.*, Eduardo V. Rodriguez, *Bankruptcy and* Individual *Chapter 11s: The Newest Battleground for the Absolute Priority Rule*, 60-FEB Fed. Law. 49 (Jan./Feb. 2013); Hon. Alan R. Jaroslovsky, United States Bankruptcy Court for the Northern District of California, Notice to Bar Regarding Individual Chapter 11 Cases, *www.canb.uscourts.gov/.../notice%20re%20chapter%2011.pdf* ("A Chapter 11 is not just a big Chapter 13.")

20 In addition, an attorney is subject to Federal Rule of Bankruptcy Procedure 9011, which requires that an attorney represent to a court that the document being filed is not being presented for an improper purpose, that the claims and defenses are warranted by existing law, and that the factual contentions and denials contained in the filings have evidentiary support.

cannot be said to have made reasonable inquiry."[21] A lawyer must also be familiar with the privacy protections afforded debtors pursuant to Federal Rule of Bankruptcy Procedure 9037. These protections include filings with redacted information and filings made under seal. A lawyer should understand the circumstances under which it is advisable for a client to take advantage of the privacy protections afforded by this Rule (including, for example, where a debtor has been subject to domestic violence, or where a minor is listed).

In addition, a lawyer must be familiar with the Electronic Case Filing ("ECF") system, and have hardware, software, and operating systems that allow for efficient access to the ECF system.[22] In addition, consistent with the ABA amendment to Comment 6 to MODEL RULE OF PROFESSIONAL CONDUCT R. 1.1, a lawyer must "keep abreast of changes in the law and its practice, including the benefits and risk associated with relevant technology. . . .[23] The recent ABA Commission on Ethics 20/20 further recognized and detailed the responsibility of lawyers with respect to technological advances and issues relating to communication and confidentiality.[24] The responsibility to acquire and maintain appropriate technological competency is relevant to lawyers practicing bankruptcy law.[25]

21 *In re* Taylor, 655 F. 3d 274, 286 (3d Cir. 2011). Although this case involved the behavior of creditor's counsel, the court was clear to observe that all attorneys in a bankruptcy case have a duty to review information provided by clients and evaluate its reasonability. Moreover, once additional information brings its reasonableness into question, attorneys has an affirmative duty to determine which facts can be reasonably supported.

22 For a cautionary tale about the misuse of the ECF system, see *In re* Smith, 462 B.R. 783 (Bankr. D. Nev. 2011) (misuse of ECF credentials).

23 American Bar Association, Commission on Ethics 20/20, Resolution adopted August 2012.

24 *Id.*

25 See In re Taylor, 655 F.3d 274 (3d. Cir. 2011). ("This case is an unfortunate example of the ways in which overreliance on computerized processes in a high-volume practice, as well as a failure on the part of clients and lawyers alike to take responsibility for accurate knowledge of a case, can lead to attorney misconduct before a court.") Id. at 277.

Because of the nature of consumer bankruptcy practices, lawyers often use subordinate lawyers and non-lawyer assistants to perform routine case-related services. Typically, in high-volume consumer bankruptcy practices, non-lawyer assistants are integral to a law firm's efficient functioning. In such cases, the senior lawyer must recognize the high level of responsibility he or she has for thoroughly training and properly supervising such subordinate lawyers and non-lawyer assistants.[26] Attention to detail is imperative in connection with debtor representation in consumer bankruptcy cases, and a lawyer's effort to keep legal fees in individual cases low by engaging in a high volume practice does not diminish a lawyer's professional responsibility to his or her client.

5. A lawyer should understand the consumer bankruptcy case process and system and have the skills to represent the debtor's interests diligently in connection with the case proceedings, keep his or her client informed, provide ongoing advice and responses to the debtor's inquiries, and be responsive to inquiries and requests made by the court and by other professionals in the case.[27]

Comment: The lawyer must be familiar with both the relevant facts of his or her client's case as well as with the applicable law. Typically, debtor representation requires a working knowledge of the Bankruptcy Code and the relevant parts of the U.S. Code addressing bankruptcy jurisdiction (Title 28) and bankruptcy crimes (Title 18); the jurisdiction's Local Rules; practice customs in the relevant jurisdiction;[28] the

26 *See* Model Rule of Professional Conduct R. 5.1 (Responsibilities of a Partner or Supervisory Lawyer).

27 See ABI Task Force on National Ethics Standards Report on Best Practices for Limited Services Representation in Consumer Bankruptcy Cases (April 2013).

28 If a lawyer practices in a district in which more than one judge sits, a lawyer is well advised to become familiar with each judge's specific style and temperament, as well as the particular requirements each judge imposes upon counsel.

Federal Rules of Bankruptcy Procedure; the Federal Rules of Evidence; state law property rules, such as Article 9 of the U.C.C. and the law regarding real property title and transfer; and state law governing domestic relations. To the extent an issue or matter arises that is outside of the bankruptcy lawyer's area of expertise (e.g., a tax or ERISA matter, or a domestic relations issue), the lawyer must seek counsel from another professional with expertise in that area.[29]

After the bankruptcy petition is filed, the case trustee sets a date for the Section 341 meeting of creditors. The lawyer should explain the process of that meeting to his or her client in order to raise issues in defense of the debtor's interests and to answer questions as they arise. Counseling at this stage in the process includes advice to debtors on the consequences of the incurring of post-petition debt.

In addition, a lawyer should be able to represent his or her client's interest in all proceedings before the bankruptcy court that are within the scope of his or her representation of the client. When appropriate in a particular case, a lawyer should have the knowledge and skills to (i) investigate and defend any avoidance actions initiated by the case trustee against the debtor, (ii) facilitate the turnover of property and documents upon the request of the trustee, (iii) appear at and represent a client's interest during a Rule 2004 examination, (iv) take steps necessary to enforce the automatic stay, including providing advice to debtors on actions for relief from stay, and (v) review reaffirmation requests and provide counsel and advice as to their advisability. A lawyer must also understand and be able to advise debtors on the extent and limits of the bankruptcy discharge, represent the debtor's interest in response to any objections contesting the discharge or the dischargeability of a particular debt, and provide counsel in the event of a violation of the discharge injunction.[30] Prior to discharge, the law-

29 *See* Model Rule R. 1.1 cmt. 2 and Model Rule 1.2 cmt. 6.

30 *See* 18 U.S.C. §§ 152–156.

yer should facilitate the client's enrollment in the Personal Financial Management course required of all consumer debtors. Throughout the case, the lawyer should respond to calls and requests for information about the case from his or her client, from other professionals in the case, including bankruptcy trustees and the United States Trustee's Office, and respond to any and all requests made by the court.[31]

Business Practice

As is true with representing consumers in bankruptcy, lawyers for business debtors must also possess certain core competencies and skills.[32] Though, on the surface, there is considerable overlap in the skills needed to represent debtors in consumer and business cases, the context in which these competencies are required and are applied can be quite different. In both types of cases, a lawyer must have an awareness of alternatives to the bankruptcy system, an understanding of bankruptcy as a substantive and procedural remedy, knowledge of the bankruptcy process, the skills to provide advice to clients in financial distress, the ability to negotiate with multiple parties with adverse interests, the organizational skills to manage an administratively complex process, the judgment to aid a client to make decisions in his best interest, and the diligence to see what can be an arduous process through to its resolution.

31 "[W]hen a person hires an attorney, he or she is entitled to a certain level of professional services and those services are to be rendered in a competent manner. An attorney should regularly communicate with his clients to insure that the clients understand the impact and scope of their case and the consequences of certain actions that may be taken in the case." In re Sledge, 352 B.R. 742, 748 (Bankr. E.D. N.C. 2006).

32 As noted above, a lawyer representing an individual in a chapter 11 cases must have knowledge of the issues need to represent debtors under both chapter 13 and chapter 11. Competent representation in an individual chapter 11 case also requires an understanding of the issues that are uniquely implicated in these cases. See Sally S. Neely, *How BAPCPA Changed Chapter 11 for Individuals, or No, This is Not Your Mother's Chapter 11* (2012).

In addition, by agreeing to represent a business bankruptcy debtor, a lawyer is representing that he or she possesses the requisite legal knowledge and skills required to navigate a business client through a reorganization or liquidation proceeding.[33] In many cases, this includes a working knowledge of finance, accounting, and asset valuation procedures. Moreover, in some types of cases, a lawyer is also representing that he or she is familiar with (or will become familiar with) the rules and practices that uniquely apply to a debtor's particular industry, market niche, or type of case (e.g., a health care industry debtor, a single-asset real estate case, or an oil and gas producer debtor). To the extent that a lawyer is not competent to provide advice and counsel with respect to an issue in connection with a business bankruptcy case (e.g., a tax matter, a stockbroker debtor, a Chapter 15 debtor's case), the lawyer must seek counsel and advice from another professional with expertise in that area.[34]

By agreeing to represent a business in connection with its bankruptcy case, the lawyer is safeguarding the trust and reliance of his or her client to provide competent representation in response to the client's oft-changing needs. The core capacities and skills possessed by a competent lawyer representing business bankruptcy clients include, but are not limited to, the following:

1. A lawyer must have the knowledge and skill to provide pre-petition operational and exit strategy counseling and information to a client or prospective client in financial distress.

33 *See* Model Rule R. 1.1 cmt. 2 and Model Rule 1.2 cmt. 6.

34 Alternatively, the lawyer can ask the client to authorize the lawyer to affiliate with another professional with the needed expertise. At the outset of an engagement, the lawyer should describe in the engagement letter the protocol to be used if it is discovered that the representation involves an issue that is outside of the lawyer's expertise. See Model Rule 1.1 cmt 2 and Model Rule 1.2 cmt. 6.

Comment: Competent handling of a business bankruptcy case begins with one or more pre-petition strategy and information sessions with a bankruptcy client (or prospective bankruptcy client).[35] A lawyer must have the depth of knowledge and experience to offer operational strategies and a sound exit plan. The lawyer should explain the myriad options and remedies available, including non-bankruptcy remedies. This discussion typically involves disclosures by the client or prospective client of financial, management and market information. The lawyer must have the skills to understand the company information, including the financial information, in order to provide useful advice as to the possible courses of action, and each course's potential consequences.

A lawyer must also make clear to the principals contemplating bankruptcy early on that the lawyer will be engaged by and will represent the debtor-in-possession and not any individual members of management.[36] The lawyer should describe the fiduciary duties of the DIP, provide examples of how the interests of the principals and the DIP may diverge, and explain what the lawyer's professional responsibilities are in such situations.[37] Finally, the lawyer should advise the principals that it might be in their best interest to engage their own counsel. The lawyer must recognize the need for a written retention letter, setting forth the scope of the representation and executed by both parties. In addition, the lawyer must be familiar with the required procedures for the retention of professionals under the Bankruptcy Code.

35 See generally, Thomas J. Salerno, et. al, Pre-Bankruptcy Planning for the Commercial Reorganization: A Guide for the CEO, CFO/COO, General Counsel and Tax Advisor (2008).

36 This of course assumes that this is the case. In the event it is not clear who the client will be prior to the lawyer's engagement, the lawyer should be mindful of any communication that may implicate issues relating to attorney-client privilege, conflicts of interest and Model Rule 1.18 governing communications with prospective clients.

37 *See* ABI Task Force on National Ethics Standards Report on Duties of Counsel for a DIP as Fiduciary and Responsibilities to the Estate (April 2013).

The lawyer must also have the requisite knowledge and skills to negotiate with some or all the client's creditors at this stage in an effort to either avert a bankruptcy filing or, in certain circumstances, to evaluate if a pre-packaged or pre-negotiated bankruptcy is feasible and advisable. In addition, the lawyer should be aware of, and communicate to his or her client, the advantages and disadvantages of: (i) liquidation, (ii) reorganization through a plan, (iii) the sale of assets under § 363 of the Bankruptcy Code, or (iv) an asset sale pursuant to a plan.

2. A lawyer should understand and be able to explain the myriad legal and business issues implicated by the prospect of a client's business bankruptcy filing. A lawyer should also be aware of the pre-petition steps required to be taken to prepare a case for filing. In addition to this substantive knowledge, a lawyer should have systems and procedures to execute the case filing efficiently and effectively.

Comment: The lawyer must have the knowledge and skills to understand and explain the issues of chapter choice and its consequences, as well as the matter of the appropriate venue and the proper timing of the filing.[38] Chapter choice requires an assessment of the client's objectives, its eligibility under each chapter, whether reorganization is desirable and feasible, and whether, if liquidation is the course of action, the case should be filed under Chapter 7, 11, 9, 12, or 15.

In addition, if the substantive and/or procedural bankruptcy law differs in the courts or jurisdictions in which a case may potentially be filed, the lawyer should be aware of these differences and make a determination, in consultation with his or her client, as to which courts or jurisdiction's laws are more in accord with his or her client's

38 A lawyer should be aware that the timing of the case must be in the best interest of the debtor and not in the best interest of the principals or other insiders. *See* Wallach v. Bucheit (*In re* Northstar Dev. Corp.), 465 B.R. 6 (Bankr. W.D.N.Y. 2012).

interests. Further, the lawyer should have the knowledge and skills to prepare a substantive analysis of the case, based on the available venue options, and taking into consideration the differences, if any, in applicable non-bankruptcy law.

The lawyer should understand the pre-bankruptcy planning steps that may need to be taken, including the identification of pre-petition financial transactions (which in turn affects the timing of the filing), a review of the firm's capital structure, and an assessment of the business's assets and liabilities. The lawyer should also be aware of the need for, and consult with his or her client about, the engagement of a claims and noticing agent, as well as the engagement of other professionals, including financial advisors and accountants. The lawyer should understand the structure of his or her entity client and obtain proper authorization to file the bankruptcy case from the appropriate client body (e.g., a corporation client's board of directors).

Moreover, the lawyer should be aware of and analyze how numerous issues may affect or be affected by the filing of the bankruptcy case. This non-exhaustive list includes:

- The necessity and availability of cash collateral;
- The necessity and availability of post-petition financing;
- The necessity and feasibility of hiring non-lawyer professionals, including financial advisors and accountants;
- The debtor's executory contracts and unexpired leases and their proposed treatment under § 365; and
- Potential avoidance actions and the likelihood, costs and benefits of their being brought.

The number and types of issues to be considered pre-filing will vary from case to case.

In addition, the lawyer must be aware of the nature and type of information and documentation necessary to be collected prior to preparing a case for filing. This information and documentation may include (depending upon the chapter selected) (a) financial statements; (b) insurance policies; (c) tax returns; (d) bank statements; (e) an inventory of all property owned by the debtor, with appropriate documentation; (f) an itemization of all debts owed by the client, with appropriate documentation; (g) real estate and mortgage information; (h) other descriptive information necessary to complete required schedules, plan and disclosure statement; and (i) identification of all going-forward expenses with appropriate detail. The lawyer must make reasonable inquiries to ensure information supplied by his or her client is accurate and complete. In the event that the lawyer recognizes an irregularity or other "red flag," he or she should be aware of the necessity of bringing the matter to the attention of his or her client, or taking other appropriate steps.[39]

Finally, the lawyer must have developed administrative systems to keep the client's information organized and accessible throughout the case. In addition, the lawyer must confirm that the client has the administrative and substantive capacity to prepare periodic financial reports, pay all interim expenses, including attorney's fees, and perform all other necessary administrative duties.

3. A lawyer should know how to prepare and file a bankruptcy petition and the related schedules and statements efficiently and effectively.

39 C.R. Bowles, Jr. & Nancy B. Rapoport, *Debtor Counsel's Fiduciary Duty: Is There a* Duty to Rat *in Chapter 11?*, 29-FEB Am. Bankr. Inst. J. 16 (2010).

Comment: Once the initial client counseling has been conducted, information and documentation gathered, and disclosures made, the lawyer must then prepare the necessary petition, schedules, statements, and forms. The lawyer must have the knowledge and skills to prepare the filing and its related schedules and statements and to conduct a reasonable inquiry into the validity and accuracy of the financial information on the Schedules and Statement of Financial Affairs provided by the client. The lawyer must understand the consequences of the timing of the case filing.

The lawyer must also be familiar with the Electronic Case Filing ("ECF") system and have hardware, software and operating systems that allow for efficient access to the ECF system.[40] Furthermore, a lawyer must "keep abreast of changes in the law and its practice, including the benefits and risk associated with relevant technology. . . .[41] The recent ABA Commission on Ethics 20/20 further recognized and detailed the responsibility of lawyers with respect to technological advances and issues relating to communication and confidentiality.[42] The responsibility to acquire and maintain appropriate technological competency is relevant to lawyers practicing business bankruptcy law. In addition, if a lawyer is aided in his or her practice by subordinate lawyers and non-lawyer assistants, the senior lawyer is responsible for thoroughly training and properly supervising such subordinate lawyers and/or non-lawyer assistants.[43]

40 For a discussion of the ramifications of abusing ECF credentials, see note 23 *supra*.

41 American Bar Association, Commission on Ethics 20/20, Resolution Adopted August 2012. For information on the Ethics 20/20 revisions involving technology, *see* http://www.americanbar.org/groups/professional_responsibility/aba_commission_on_ethics_20_20/house_of_delegates_filings.html.

42 *See* American Bar Association, Commission on Ethics 20/20, Resolution Adopted August 2012.

43 *See* Model Rule of Professional Conduct R. 5.1 (Responsibilities of a Partner or Supervisory Lawyer).

4. Lawyers must be aware of and comply with the provisions of the Bankruptcy Code and related rules relevant during the immediate post-filing time period. A lawyer should have the knowledge and skills to argue first-day motions and otherwise take steps to address the substantive and procedural issues that arise at the beginning of a case.

Comment: The business bankruptcy lawyer must be familiar with both the relevant facts of his or her client's case as well as with the applicable law. Typically, debtor representation requires a working knowledge of the Bankruptcy Code and the relevant parts of the U.S. Code addressing bankruptcy jurisdiction (Title 28) and bankruptcy crimes (Title 18); the jurisdiction's Local Rules; practice customs in the relevant jurisdiction;[44] the Federal Rules of Bankruptcy Procedure; the Federal Rules of Evidence; state law property rules, such as Article 9 of the U.C.C. and the law regarding real property title and transfer; and state law governing domestic relations. To the extent an issue or matter arises that is outside of the bankruptcy lawyer's area of expertise or implicates issues that are less commonly encountered, (such as stockbroker debtors, railroads, health care facilities, Chapter 15 cases, Chapter 12 cases, tax and ERISA matters, to name a few), the lawyer should gain an understanding of the relevant issues, or seek counsel from a professional with experience and expertise in the issue or matter.

In addition to being a skilled advisor, negotiator and drafter, in many cases lawyers for debtors in possession must also have the ability to advocate for their clients in bankruptcy court. In a Chapter 11 case, the lawyer typically addresses his or her client's exigent issues by arguing "first-day motions."[45] By way of illustration, these motions may include:

44 If a lawyer practices in a district in which more than one judge sits, a lawyer is well advised to become familiar with each judge's specific style and temperament, as well as the particular requirements each judge imposes upon counsel.

45 American Bankruptcy Institute, First Day Motions (2010).

- A motion to employ counsel and other professionals (this process involves the disclosure of connections, as set forth in Rule 2014);
- A motion to extend time to file schedules and statements;
- A motion to retain "ordinary course professionals";
- A motion to authorize procedures for notice;
- A motion to approve investment guidelines;
- A motion to apply cash management procedures;
- A motion to obtain post-petition financing;
- A motion to establish interim professional fees procedures;
- A motion to use cash collateral;
- A motion to pay pre-petition employee wages; and
- A motion to honor pre-petition obligations to vendors and taxing authorities.

A lawyer must be aware of and communicate the numerous issues necessary to be addressed on an exigent basis in each individual case and have the skill to argue in support of his or her client's interests. Moreover, the lawyer must be aware of and comply with the applicable operational provisions in the Bankruptcy Code and related Rules, such as certain required notices, disclosures, and filings. These include the noticing rules for motions that must be sent to appropriate parties. The applicability of many of these requirements turns on the nature, size, and type of business case.

In addition, a lawyer for a business DIP must have the knowledge and skills to:

- Facilitate the turnover of property and documents upon request of parties in interest;
- Take steps necessary to enforce the automatic stay, including providing advice to the client on actions for relief from stay;
- Represent his or her client's interests in connection with objections to claims;
- Represent the debtor in possession at the Section 341 meeting; and
- Appear and represent his or her client's interests at Rule 2004 examinations.

A lawyer must provide continuing disclosures to the court, as necessary (e.g., Rule 2014 disclosures).[46] A lawyer must also respond to calls and requests from his or her client, the court, and creditors and other parties in interest, including bankruptcy trustees and the United States Trustee.

5. The lawyer representing a reorganizing DIP must have the knowledge and skills to draft an effective and confirmable plan of reorganization and disclosure statement in compliance with the relevant Bankruptcy Code provisions.

Comment: If a plan is to be drafted, it must satisfy the requirements of Chapter 11 and, more specifically, the plan confirmation requirements of Section 1129(a). This requires the lawyer's familiarity with

46 *See* ABI Report of ABI Task Force on Proposed Amendment to Rule 2014 (April 2013).

the nuances for structuring a plan, including the classification of claims, and the satisfaction of the "best interests" test (which in turn requires a liquidation and feasibility analysis). The lawyer must further understand the various methods used to value assets, and be able to assess any such valuations. In addition, the lawyer for the DIP must be familiar with bankruptcy procedure, including the timing of key events in the case, such as the exclusivity period, the deadline for filing a disclosure statement and plan, the timing of vote solicitation, and the confirmation hearing.

The lawyer must also have the knowledge and skills to draft a disclosure statement, which must include thorough and complete information about the proposed plan and its consequences. A lawyer must understand the required standards for disclosure in order to solicit plan votes effectively. In the case of a publicly held DIP, the lawyer should also follow the applicable securities laws.

6. A lawyer should have the substantive and procedural knowledge and skills to manage the bankruptcy case and to effectively represent his or her client in all case proceedings.

Comment: The business bankruptcy lawyer must be aware of the range of matters that may need to be addressed throughout the pendency of the case and must possess the skills and experience to address them. An illustrative list includes:

- The consideration of whether to accept or reject executory contracts and the relevant rules with respect to the timing of such actions;

- Ongoing assessments of cash collateral availability and need;

- Ongoing assessments of post-petition financing availability and need;

- The providing of advice concerning retaining non-lawyer professionals;
- The pursuit of any avoidance actions determined to be in the client's interest; and
- The monitoring of the DIP's ongoing financial performance.

7. A lawyer must be aware of the need to offer his or her client ongoing advice and provide the court with relevant disclosures throughout the duration of the bankruptcy case.

Comment: During the pendency of the case, the lawyer should continue to confer with and respond to inquiries from his or her client and provide proactive assistance with respect to the DIP's fulfillment of its fiduciary duties to the estate. In addition, a lawyer must be aware of his or her duty to comply proactively with any reporting requirements imposed by the court and by the Office of the United States Trustee.

8. The lawyer should have knowledge and understanding of the process of getting retained by the client, as well as the procedures required to be followed in order to receive professional fees. In addition, the lawyer must ensure that other professionals in the case understand the retention and payment requirements imposed by the Bankruptcy Code.

Comment: As an estate professional, the lawyer for the DIP must understand the process of retention, how time is to be billed, and the procedure necessary to be followed in order to have fees approved by the court. This includes the proper structure and use of pre-petition retainers and payments of pre petition fees (or waiver of claims for such fees) to preserve continued employability and disinterestedness. In addition, a DIP's lawyer must ensure that any non-bankruptcy professionals, such as securities or corporate counsel, financial advisors, accountants and real estate agents, and fellow professionals within the lawyer's own firm understand the particulars of the bankruptcy retention and fee application process.

9. A lawyer must have the knowledge and skill to provide his or her client with advice concerning plan confirmation and the post-confirmation injunction.

Comment: A lawyer must understand and advise debtors on the extent and limits of the bankruptcy discharge and represent the debtor's interest in response to any objections contesting the discharge.[47] In addition, the lawyer must counsel the debtor about the scope of, and if necessary, respond to actions in violation of the post-confirmation injunction.

Maintaining Competence

As Comment 6 to ABA Model Rule 1.1 observes, "[t]o maintain the requisite knowledge and skill, a lawyer should keep abreast of changes in the law and its practice, including the benefits and risk associated with relevant technology, engage in continuing study and education and comply with all continuing legal education requirements to which the lawyer is subject."

- In the field of bankruptcy, lawyers must be aware of new developments in both statutory and case law. Lawyers should remain cognizant of any changes to the Official Forms and be aware of changes to federal and local rules of procedure and evidence. Lawyers should also be familiar with changes and developments in relevant technology.[48]

47 *See* 11 U.S.C. § 523; *see also* 18 U.S.C. §§ 152–156.

48 American Bar Association, Commission on Ethics 20/20, Resolution adopted August 2012.

- A lawyer representing debtors in both consumer and business cases should adhere to the requirements for admission and continued practice established by local bankruptcy courts.

- A lawyer representing consumer debtors, business debtors, or DIPs should participate in relevant continuing education courses.

- A lawyer desiring to begin a practice representing consumer debtors should participate in education courses, mentoring, and/or individual instruction prior to preparing cases for filing.

- A lawyer desiring to begin practice representing business debtors should similarly participate in education courses and, preferably, gain experience working under the supervision of more experienced attorneys.

Proposed Rule

PROPOSED BANKRUPTCY RULE [ADMINISTRATIVE ORDER]
GOVERNING THE ADMISSION AND PRACTICE
OF PRIMARY ATTORNEYS IN BANKRUPTCY
COURT PROCEEDINGS

1.1 An attorney is qualified for admission to and practice in this Court as primary bankruptcy attorney for a party in interest if the attorney:

(a) is currently a member in good standing of the State Bar of ____________ and the Bar of the United States District Court for the __________ District of __________; and

(b) certifies that he/she has, and will maintain, a working knowledge of this Court's local rules and administrative orders, the relevant provisions of Title 28 (bankruptcy jurisdiction), the Bankruptcy Code, all of the applicable federal rules of procedure and evidence, Title 18 (bankruptcy crimes), and the Rules of Professional Conduct of the State Bar and any other state bar of which the attorney is a member, and will reasonably supervise the work of others working for with him/her in the representation.

1.2 By appearing in matters before this Court, a primary bankruptcy attorney is continually certifying that, during the past two years, he/she has completed at least ten hours of continuing legal education in the areas of Federal Bankruptcy Law and relevant federal and state law and at least two hours of continuing legal education in bankruptcy-related ethics or has associated with an attorney who makes such a certification.

1.3 In order to represent debtors in bankruptcy cases, the attorney's working knowledge should demonstrate competence requisite to the nature of the case being filed. It may be necessary for an attorney to associate with an attorney who has demonstrated such appropriate working knowledge.

1.4 This rule is not intended to preclude an attorney who is not qualified as a primary bankruptcy attorney from giving emergency representation to a party in interest as long as such representation is limited to that which is reasonably necessary under the circumstances.

1.5 Attorneys residing in other jurisdictions who do not meet the requirements of 1.1(a) may be admitted pro hac vice pursuant to Local Rule/Order ______.

Appendix B—Time Sheet

DATE	CLIENT NAME	CLIENT BILLING NO.	DESCRIPTION OF WORK	TIME SPENT

Appendix C

Florida State Constitution, Article X, Section 4

SECTION 4. Homestead; exemptions.—

(a) There shall be exempt from forced sale under process of any court, and no judgment, decree or execution shall be a lien thereon, except for the payment of taxes and assessments thereon, obligations contracted for the purchase, improvement or repair thereof, or obligations contracted for house, field or other labor performed on the realty, the following property owned by a natural person:

(1) a homestead, if located outside a municipality, to the extent of one hundred sixty acres of contiguous land and improvements thereon, which shall not be reduced without the owner's consent by reason of subsequent inclusion in a municipality; or if located within a municipality, to the extent of one-half acre of contiguous land, upon which the exemption shall be limited to the residence of the owner or the owner's family;

(2) personal property to the value of one thousand dollars.

(b) These exemptions shall inure to the surviving spouse or heirs of the owner.

(c) The homestead shall not be subject to devise if the owner is survived by spouse or minor child, except the homestead may be devised to the owner's spouse if there be no minor child. The owner of homestead real estate, joined by the spouse if married, may alienate the homestead by mortgage, sale or gift and, if married, may by deed transfer the title to an estate by the entirety with the spouse. If the owner or spouse is incompetent, the method of alienation or encumbrance shall be as provided by law.

History.—Am. H.J.R. 4324, 1972; adopted 1972; Am. H.J.R. 40, 1983; adopted 1984; Am. proposed by Constitution Revision Commission, Revision No. 13, 1998, filed with the Secretary of State May 5, 1998; adopted 1998.

Florida Statutes Annotated

222.01 Designation of homestead by owner before levy.—

(1) Whenever any natural person residing in this state desires to avail himself or herself of the benefit of the provisions of the constitution and laws exempting property as a homestead from forced sale under any process of law, he or she may make a statement, in writing, containing a description of the real property, mobile home, or modular home claimed to be exempt and declaring that the real property, mobile home, or modular home is the homestead of the party in whose behalf such claim is being made. Such statement shall be signed by the person making it and shall be recorded in the circuit court.

(2) When a certified copy of a judgment has been filed in the public records of a county pursuant to chapter 55, a person who is entitled to the benefit of the provisions of the State Constitution exempting real property as homestead and who has a contract to sell or a commitment from a lender for a mortgage on the homestead may file a notice of homestead in the public records of the county in which the homestead property is located in substantially the following form:

NOTICE OF HOMESTEAD

To: (*Name and address of judgment creditor as shown on recorded judgment and name and address of any other person shown in the recorded judgment to receive a copy of the Notice of Homestead*).

You are notified that the undersigned claims as homestead exempt from levy and execution under Section 4, Article X of the State Constitution, the following described property:

(Legal description)

The undersigned certifies, under oath, that he or she has applied for and received the homestead tax exemption as to the above-described property, that is the tax identification parcel number of this property, and that the undersigned has resided on this property continuously and uninterruptedly from (date) to the date of this Notice of Homestead. Further, the undersigned will either convey or mortgage the above-described property pursuant to the following:

(Describe the contract of sale or loan commitment by date, names of parties, date of anticipated closing, and amount. The name, address, and telephone number of the person conducting the anticipated closing must be set forth.)

The undersigned also certifies, under oath, that the judgment lien filed by you on (date) and recorded in Official Records Book ___, Page ___, of the Public Records of___ County, Florida, does not constitute a valid lien on the described property.

YOU ARE FURTHER NOTIFIED, PURSUANT TO SECTION 222.01 ET SEQ., FLORIDA STATUTES, THAT WITHIN 45 DAYS AFTER THE MAILING OF THIS NOTICE YOU MUST FILE AN ACTION IN THE CIRCUIT COURT OF___COUNTY, FLORIDA,

FOR A DECLARATORY JUDGMENT TO DETERMINE THE CONSTITUTIONAL HOMESTEAD STATUS OF THE SUBJECT PROPERTY OR TO FORECLOSE YOUR JUDGMENT LIEN ON THE PROPERTY AND RECORD A LIS PENDENS IN THE PUBLIC RECORDS OF THE COUNTY WHERE THE HOMESTEAD IS LOCATED. YOUR FAILURE TO SO ACT WILL RESULT IN ANY BUYER OR LENDER, OR HIS OR HER SUCCESSORS AND ASSIGNS, UNDER THE ABOVE-DESCRIBED CONTRACT OF SALE OR LOAN COMMITMENT TO TAKE FREE AND CLEAR OF ANY JUDGMENT LIEN YOU MAY HAVE ON THE PROPERTY.

This___day of ______, 2 ___.

____

(Signature of Owner)

____

____

(Printed Name of Owner)

____

____

(Owner's Address)

____

Sworn to and subscribed before me by who is personally known to me or produced as identification, this ___ day of ______, ____.

____

Notary Public

(3) The clerk shall mail a copy of the notice of homestead to the judgment lienor, by certified mail, return receipt requested, at the address shown in the most recent recorded judgment or accompanying affidavit, and to any other person designated in the most recent recorded judgment or accompanying affidavit to receive the notice of homestead, and shall certify to such service on the face of such notice and record the notice. Notwithstanding the use of certified mail, return receipt requested, service shall be deemed complete upon mailing.

(4) A lien pursuant to chapter 55 of any lienor upon whom such notice is served, who fails to institute an action for a declaratory judgment to determine the constitutional homestead status of the property described in the notice of homestead or to file an action to foreclose the judgment lien, together with the filing of a lis pendens in the public records of the county in which the homestead is located, within 45 days after service of such notice shall be deemed as not attaching to the property by virtue of its status as homestead property as to the interest of any buyer or lender, or his or her successors or assigns, who takes under the contract of sale or loan commitment described above within 180 days after the filing in the public records of the notice of homestead. This subsection shall not act to prohibit a lien from attaching to the real property described in the notice of homestead at such time as the property loses its homestead status.

(5) As provided in s. 4, Art. X of the State Constitution, this subsection shall not apply to:

(a) Liens and judgments for the payment of taxes and assessments on real property.

(b) Liens and judgments for obligations contracted for the purchase of real property.

(c) Liens and judgments for labor, services, or materials furnished to repair or improve real property.

(d) Liens and judgments for other obligations contracted for house, field, or other labor performed on real property.

History.—s. 1, ch. 1715, 1869; RS 1998; GS 2520; RGS 3875; CGL 5782; s. 20, ch. 73-334; s. 2, ch. 77-299; s. 1, ch. 83-40; s. 1195, ch. 95-147; s. 25, ch. 2000-258; s. 17, ch. 2005-241.

222.02 Designation of homestead after levy.—Whenever a levy is made upon the lands, tenements, mobile home, or modular home of such person whose homestead has not been set apart and selected, such person, or the person's agent or attorney, may in writing notify the officer making such levy, by notice under oath made before any officer of this state duly authorized to administer oaths, at any time before the day appointed for the sale thereof, of what such person regards as his or her homestead, with a description thereof; and the remainder only shall be subject to sale under such levy.

History.—s. 2, ch. 1715, 1869; RS 1999; GS 2521; RGS 3876; CGL 5783; s. 3, ch. 77-299; s. 2, ch. 83-40; s. 1196, ch. 95-147.

* * *

222.05 Setting apart leasehold.—Any person owning and occupying any dwelling house, including a mobile home used as a residence, or modular home, on land not his or her own which he or she may lawfully possess, by lease or otherwise, and claiming such house, mobile home, or modular home as his or her homestead, shall be entitled to the exemption of such house, mobile home, or modular home from levy and sale as aforesaid.

History.—s. 5, ch. 1715, 1869; RS 2002; GS 2524; RGS 3879; CGL 5786; s. 1, ch. 77-299; s. 1198, ch. 95-147.

Texas State Constitution

Article 16—GENERAL PROVISIONS

Section 50—HOMESTEAD; PROTECTION FROM FORCED SALE; MORTGAGES, TRUST DEEDS, AND LIENS

(a) The homestead of a family, or of a single adult person, shall be, and is hereby protected from forced sale, for the payment of all debts except for:

(1) the purchase money thereof, or a part of such purchase money;

(2) the taxes due thereon; * * *

Texas Statutes Annotated

SUBTITLE A. PROPERTY EXEMPT FROM CREDITORS' CLAIMSCHAPTER 41. INTERESTS IN LANDSUBCHAPTER A. EXEMPTIONS IN LAND DEFINED

§ 41.001. INTERESTS IN LAND EXEMPT FROM SEIZURE

(a) A homestead and one or more lots used for a place of burial of the dead are exempt from seizure for the claims of creditors except for encumbrances properly fixed on homestead property.

(b) Encumbrances may be properly fixed on homestead property for:

(1) purchase money;

(2) taxes on the property;

(3) work and material used in constructing improvements on the property if contracted for in writing as provided by Sections 53.254(a), (b), and (c);

(4) an owelty of partition imposed against the entirety of the property by a court order or by a written agreement of the parties to the partition, including a debt of one spouse in favor of the other spouse resulting from a division or an award of a family homestead in a divorce proceeding;

(5) the refinance of a lien against a homestead, including a federal tax lien resulting from the tax debt of both spouses, if the homestead is a family homestead, or from the tax debt of the owner;

(6) an extension of credit that meets the requirements of Section 50(a)(6), Article XVI, Texas Constitution; or

(7) a reverse mortgage that meets the requirements of Sections 50(k)-(p), Article XVI, Texas Constitution.

(c) The homestead claimant›s proceeds of a sale of a homestead are not subject to seizure for a creditor›s claim for six months after the date of sale.

Amended by Acts 1985, 69th Leg., ch. 840, § 1, eff. June 15, 1985; Acts 1993, 73rd Leg., ch. 48, § 2, eff. Sept. 1, 1993; Acts 1995, 74th Leg., ch. 121, § 1.01, eff. May 17, 1995; Acts 1995, 74th Leg., ch. 121, § 2.01; Acts 1997, 75th Leg., ch. 526, § 1, eff. Sept. 1,1997; Acts 2001, 77th Leg., ch. 516, § 1, eff. Sept. 1, 2001.

§ 41.002. DEFINITION OF HOMESTEAD

(a) If used for the purposes of an urban home or as both an urban home and a place to exercise a calling or business, the homestead of a family or a single, adult person, not otherwise entitled to a homestead, shall consist of not more than 10 acres of land which may be in one or more contiguous lots, together with any improvements thereon.

* * *

(c) A homestead is considered to be urban if, at the time the designation is made, the property is:

(1) located within the limits of a municipality or its extraterritorial jurisdiction or a platted subdivision; and

(2) served by police protection, paid or volunteer fire protection, and at least three of the following services provided by a municipality or under contract to a municipality:

(A) electric;

(B) natural gas;

(C) sewer;

(D) storm sewer; and

(E) water.

(d) The definition of a homestead as provided in this section applies to all homesteads in this state whenever created.

Amended by Acts 1985, 69th Leg., ch. 840, § 1, eff. June 15, 1985; Acts 1989, 71st Leg., ch. 391, § 2, eff. Aug. 28, 1989; Acts 1999, 76th Leg., ch. 1510, § 1, eff. Jan. 1, 2000; Acts 1999, 76th Leg., ch. 1510, § 2, eff. Sept. 1, 1999.